THE CHALLENGE

Transforming the World Through Covenant Living

David Edwards

LifeWay Christian Resources
Nashville, Tennessee

Produced by:
National Collegiate Ministry Department
LifeWay Christian Resources
127 Ninth Avenue, North
Nashville, Tennessee 37234-0153
Customer Service: (800) 458-2772

Editor: Art Herron
Production Specialist: Leanne Lawrence
Art Director: Edward Crawford

© Copyright 2000 LifeWay Press
All rights reserved.
Printed in the United States of America.

ISBN 0-7673-9295-7

CrossSeekers®, CrossSeekers logo, CrossSeekers person figure, and the six Covenant icons are all trademarks of LifeWay Christian Resources.
All rights reserved.

Dewey Decimal Classification: 248.834
Subject Heading: SPIRITUAL LIFE

Unless otherwise noted, all Scripture quotations are taken from the Holy Bible, *New International Version*, copyright © 1973, 1978, 1984 by International Bible Society. Used by permission.

Scripture marked NASB is taken from the *NEW AMERICAN STANDARD BIBLE*, © Copyright The Lockman Foundation, 1960, 1962, 1963, 1968, 1971, 1972, 1973, 1975, 1977, 1995
Used by permission.

Order additional copies of this book by writing to Customer Service Center, MSN 113; 127 Ninth Avenue, North; Nashville, TN 37234-0113; by calling toll free (800) 458-2772; by faxing (615) 251-5933; by ordering online at www.lifeway.com; by emailing customerservice@lifeway.com; or by visiting a LifeWay Christian Store.

LifeWay Press
127 Ninth Avenue North
Nashville, Tennessee 37234-0152

As God works through us, we will help people and churches know Jesus Christ and seek His kingdom by providing biblical solutions that spiritually transform individuals and cultures.

Leader's Guide—Group Study

A leader's guide is available at no cost if you are leading a group study of this resource. If you need one or more copies, please contact National Collegiate Ministry in Nashville, Tennessee. Our number is 615-251-2777 (CST). Our mailing address is 127 Ninth Ave., North, Nashville, TN 37234-0153.

contents

about the writer 4

the crossseekers covenant 6

introduction 7

session one
hope, not hype: the meaning of the covenant 10

session two
just one thing: the single plan of history 22

session three
the truth behind performance: the life of integrity 34

session four
cold water crossing: the resilient advance of the spirit . . . 50

session five
transforming the world: it takes more than a t-shirt . . . 66

session six
brick by brick: building the house of God 80

session seven
dispossess to possess: the cycle of purity 94

session eight
no more tears: the power of covenant friendship 108

resources 126

The Challenge
Transforming the World
Through Covenant Living

about the writer

David Edwards speaks from his heart about issues relevant to university students. He is the featured speaker for METRO Bible Study at Germantown Baptist Church in Memphis, TN and METRO Bible Study held at First Baptist Church, Orlando, FL. He was the founding speaker for METRO Bible Study held at First Baptist Church, Houston, TX. He travels full time speaking on college campuses, retreats, revivals, and summer camps.

David graduated from Oklahoma City University with a B.A. in Religious Education and completed his work toward a masters from Southwestern Baptist Theological Seminary, Ft. Worth, Texas.

David's mission is to "reintroduce the truth of God's Word by meeting people where they are in life and bringing them **one step close**r in the process of knowing and becoming like Jesus Christ."

David is author of the book, *One Step Closer*, creator and speaker for the DESTINATION video series: *Principles for Making Life's Journey Count*, author of the witnessing booklet, *How to Make Life All Good*, and author of the CrossSeekers book *Holy and Acceptable, Building a Pure Temple*. He writes for *Christian Single* and *Living Solo* magazines.

acknowledgments

To those who BROUGHT me into covenant: Dr. Jay Strack, Ms. Flo Flickie, John Bullard, Craig Groeschell, Andy Savage and Memphis METRO Bible Study.

To those who SOUGHT me in covenant: Dr. Anthony Jordan, Kyle McDaniel and Generation Reformation. I wrote this book on your gift. Jay Bruce, you are a true Amerikano, Bobby McGraw—for working the late shift, and The Alman Brothers.

To those who TAUGHT me covenant: Andy Stanley and Lanny Donoho.

My "Paul," R.H. In searching for words which express appreciation for your love and the impact you've made in my life, I can only think of a line from the song "The Leader of the Band":
"My life has been a poor attempt to imitate THE MAN. I'm just a living legacy of the Leader of the Band."

The CrossSeekers® Covenant

"You will seek me and find me when you seek me with all your heart." Jeremiah 29:13

As a seeker of the cross of Christ, I am called to break away from trite, nonchalant, laissez-faire Christian living. I accept the challenge to divine daring, to consecrated recklessness for Christ, to devout adventure in the face of ridiculing contemporaries. I acknowledge I am created in the image of God and am committed to excellence as a disciple of Jesus Christ.

INTEGRITY

I will seek to be a person of integrity

"Do your best to present yourself to God as one approved, a workman who does not need to be ashamed and who correctly handles the word of truth." 2 Timothy 2:15

My attitudes and actions reveal my commitment to live the kind of life Christ modeled for me—to speak the truth in love, to stand firm in my convictions, to be honest and trustworthy.

SPIRITUAL GROWTH

I will seek to pursue consistent spiritual growth

"So then, just as you received Christ Jesus as Lord, continue to live in him, rooted and built up in him, strengthened in the faith as you were taught, and overflowing with thankfulness." Colossians 2:6-7

The Christian life is a continuing journey, and I am committed to a consistent, personal relationship with Jesus Christ, to faithful study of His Word, and to regular corporate spiritual growth through the ministry of the New Testament church.

WITNESS

I will seek to speak and live a relevant, authentic, and consistent witness

"Always be prepared to give an answer to everyone who asks you to give the reason for the hope that you have." 1 Peter 3:15

I will tell others the story of how Jesus changed my life, and I will seek to live a radically changed life each day. I will share the good news of Jesus Christ with courage and boldness.

SERVICE

I will seek opportunities to serve in Christ's name

"The Spirit of the Lord is on me, because he has anointed me to preach good news to the poor. He has sent me to proclaim freedom for the prisoners and recovery of sight for the blind, to release the oppressed, to proclaim the year of the Lord's favor." Luke 4:18-19

I believe that God desires to draw all people into a loving, redeeming relationship with Him. As His disciple, I will give myself to be His hands to reach others in ministry and missions.

PURITY

I will seek to honor my body as the temple of God, dedicated to a lifestyle of purity

"Do you not know that your body is a temple of the Holy Spirit, who is in you, whom you have received from God? You are not your own; you were bought at a price. Therefore honor God with your body." 1 Corinthians 6:19-20

Following the example of Christ, I will keep my body healthy and strong, avoiding temptations and destructive personal vices. I will honor the gift of life by keeping myself sexually pure and free from addictive drugs.

CHRISTLIKE RELATIONSHIPS

I will seek to be godly in all things, Christlike in all relationships

"Therefore, as God's chosen people, holy and dearly loved, clothe yourselves with compassion, kindness, humility, gentleness and patience. Bear with each other and forgive whatever grievances you may have against one another. Forgive as the Lord forgave you. And over all these virtues put on love, which binds them all together in perfect unity." Colossians 3:12-14

In every relationship and in every situation, I will seek to live as Christ would. I will work to heal brokenness, to value each person as a child of God, to avoid petty quarrels and harsh words, to let go of bitterness and resentment that hinder genuine Christian love.

Copyright © 1998 LifeWay Publications. CrossSeekers is a ministry of National Collegiate Ministry. For more information, visit our Web site: www.crossseekers.org.

The Challenge
Transforming the World Through Covenant Living

introduction

College can be some of the best four to twelve years of your life. Sure there's the course load, but for most of us that commands about as much interest as belly button lint. Basically, college is summer camp with money. You spend all your time in a beer-infested campus, surrounded by the smell of bong water and last night's pizza—and that's if you're at a spiritually conservative college.

I am not bashing college life. (Part of the reason I'm a minister is so I can keep college hours!) Maybe you don't drink and don't party. You haven't joined your local fraternity. (Perhaps you rushed but didn't get in.) Maybe you have been part of one of the Christian clubs, and over the semester, you've become proficient at the art of ping-pong. Bring it on Forrest, you're mine.

But surely college should be something more than just summer camp with money, shouldn't it? If we are not careful, college can become a state of arrested adolescence. **We postpone maturity, and in the process we miss some of life's most important lessons—especially the spiritual ones.**

I remember where I was when I realized that students might not be seeing the whole picture of the Christian life. I had just finished speaking at a major Christian college, and I sat down with the minister of students to have a soda (which, by the way, is especially tasty after an awesome match of ping-pong). I was going to do a CrossSeekers conference there that evening. Slurping on his soda, the minister of students remarked, "You know CrossSeekers is good, but all they are really doing is basically asking students to witness, pray, and have a quiet time, and my students are already doing that." It's just things to do!

I thought to myself, "Crush some more tinfoil on the antennae, 'cause you are getting a bad reception." This guy had no idea what CrossSeekers is asking people to do. At that moment, this book was born in my heart.

I believe this minister is not alone. He, like many others, thinks of Christianity as a list of things to do.

In the Old Testament there was a list of things to do—go to the temple, make sacrifices, burn incense, etc. Today, some of our Christian calisthenics are just an updated version of those things. But that attitude has nothing to do with covenant. It sounds more like a contract to me. Covenant is about relationship, and for too long the church has told people what to do in their lives with God, without giving them God's rationale. That is the focus of this book and the focus of CrossSeekers.

This book says that if you read the Bible to cop a wicked theological revelation but miss the Christ walking off of every page, then you need more tinfoil on your antennae. *CrossSeekers is not about doing; it's about relationship.*

And that's what this book is about—relationship. We must remember that our relationship with God was made available to us only because Jesus fulfilled God's covenant with Abraham. Knowing that God did all of the work should free us from trying to prove our worth by our actions. That's the message that Paul gives in Galatians 3 when he asks, "Are you so foolish? Having begun by the Spirit, are you now being perfected by the flesh?" (Gal. 3:3).

So listen up collegians: let me tell you that CrossSeekers is not a knock-off of some other student ministry. It is not the enemy of any other ministry that has a kingdom mentality. It was not started out of comparison or envy. It is unique in its focus, in that **CrossSeekers is about covenant living**. Covenant living is different. Christian living for some means embracing Christian principles; **covenant living is about embracing the person of Jesus Christ.** Only this relationship can open up a clearer vision of the heart of God towards us and the rule of God in the midst of the details of our lives.

This book is not an in-depth study into all of the covenants in the Bible. Rather, it contains an introduction to covenant living in chapters 1 and 2, followed by the application of the covenant principles in the six areas of the CrossSeekers statements. I believe that the six CrossSeekers statements represent what will flow out of your relationship with God—not silly church rules that you promise to keep today, but forget tomorrow. There's nothing magical about the order or the wording of the CrossSeekers Covenant, but if you can't see these things naturally flowing out of your life with God, there's something wrong.

Imagine: Transforming the world—covenant people establishing the righteousness of God by regularly intersecting the lives of others in their communities with the life-giving presence of the covenant God. They extend the rule of God throughout the world by building a covenant community of people characterized by freedom, strength, and celebration.

This book is a call to you to discern your place in that community. I hope that what you read stirs you and stretches you. I pray that it will shake you up. I pray that it will shake up your religious spirit and revive the heartbeat of Christ within you.

Remember, if you are leading a group study, a free leader's guide is available by calling 615-251-2777.

Hope, Not Hype: The Meaning of the Covenant

The Challenge
Transforming the World Through Covenant Living

Hope, Not Hype: The Meaning of the Covenant

"New and improved." "Bigger and better than ever." "Too good to be true." That's right—they are synonyms for *hype*. This four-letter word means "to build something on nothing," and it is impacting our lives more than we realize.

Take computers. The ads say they are fun because you can "surf" the Internet. Please tell me how sitting in front of a screen and pecking at keys like a trained chicken has anything to do with surfing.

And the tabloids have subscribers. Can you believe that? Those papers are so bad birds won't use them.

On TV, the late night sell-salesman de jour hypes the latest must-have exercise machine that promises you a body that can pull a truck after you use a piece of equipment that's little more than a mechanics creeper and a string. There's also the get-rich-quick book which makes only the writer rich, quick. And so the spin continues: the food dehydrator, costume jewelry, and knives that can saw a can in half.

I know people in glass houses shouldn't throw stones, and though mine has stained glass, it doesn't filter out the fact that the cheap light of hype has found its way into Christianity.

For instance: WWJD mace? The story of the Prodigal son printed on frisbees? (Shouldn't it be printed on a boom-a-rang?)

Then there's Easter. What does the death and resurrection of Christ have to do with a bunny and eggs? I've figured it out. The twelve eggs in a carton are the twelve disciples. And there's always that cracked one. That is the evil Judas egg.

We may laugh at these things (I sure do!), but we must admit that they are symptomatic of a superficial Christianity and a shallow faith. All of the smoke and mirrors of hype have clouded our hope. We need to reacquaint ourselves with the elements of our hope, because our hope is no hype.

Hope Beyond the Hype
A covenantal biography
Soon after the death of Manasseh, his son Amon took the throne. The entire kingdom was the heartland of pagan worship, and Amon himself

worshiped the god of Assyria. The gods of Canaan were worshiped as well.

Amon held the throne just two years. His enemies slashed his throat, and as he lay in a pool of his own blood, another successor was chosen. The high-ranking officials crowned Amon's eight-year-old son, Josiah, the next king.

By the time Josiah turned twenty-one, he was truly a king. After a successful military campaign, Josiah ruled with confidence. During this period, his heart was changed with a defining moment. The voice of a prophet named Jeremiah tore through the pagan air with the very words of God: "The people of Judah have done evil in my eyes, declares the Lord. They have set up their detestable idols in the house that bears my Name and have defiled it" (Jer. 7:30).

For the next five years he bothered and frightened the people of Jerusalem with his scathing words, until one day things were different. Josiah had cleaned out the pagan high places of worship with its priests and prostitutes, and he had destroyed the Asherrah.

Josiah remembered Jeremiah's words of warning, and he knew that purging the land wasn't good enough. Josiah's grandfather, Manasseh, had died when he was six. Josiah remembered that Manasseh underwent a personal revival. Taken into captivity, he cried out for the Lord, and the Lord revived his heart. He returned to the city, but he did not live long enough for his personal revival to affect the nation.

Josiah spent hours reading the journals of David, and the words of David touched him. He longed to be a king like David had been king. The sun hung high over Jerusalem, and from his terrace Josiah could see the city. In the center was the temple. Its great spires reflected the sun and pierced through the sky. "That's it," he thought to himself. "The temple, the heart of worship, the place of God, the dream of David. I will open it once again."

The temple had been closed for 75 years, and it was obvious that no one ever stopped to notice it. Josiah had a big task ahead.

Now 26, Josiah initiated the cleaning and the repairing of the temple. It was during this restoration that a long scroll was found. It was a book of the Law. Shaphan, the secretary for Josiah, brought it immediately to the king. "Josiah," he said, "the priests have found an old scroll." Josiah looked at him from his throne and said, "Read it." Shaphan then read the entire book aloud. It was God's covenant with Moses. Sinai unfolded there before him. This was God's Word spoken before David and before Jerusalem ever was.

Josiah had discovered the covenant. What God had said to Israel through the covenant was basically, "Follow Me as Lord and My blessings will be upon you. Disobey Me and you will suffer the consequences" (see Deut. 28). Josiah knew that those words given to Moses and the people were still valid for him and his people. He knew that he, his father, his grandfather, and all of the people of the kingdom had been living in violation of the covenant.

Josiah gathered the priests, the elders, and all the citizens and read the covenant aloud. As they listened and watched, Josiah made a covenant with the Lord: to keep His commandments and to live out the covenant words of the Lord.

All the people committed themselves to the covenant by walking through the blood between the two halves of a goat and a heifer. As they walked, they were embracing the covenant for themselves. What followed was a 40-year revival in the hearts of the people. God was the only focus of worship, and this was the covenant renewal.

Now the idea of covenant may be unknown to you. Even as I type this into my computer, the spell check does not recognize "covenantal," and many of us are equally unfamiliar with the words "covenant" and "covenantal," as well as the principles. So, like Josiah, there must be a covenant revival in our lives.

The things Josiah discovered about the covenants are the things you and I need to discover. Nothing will have a greater impact on the way you do life. These simple, yet profound, principles will increase your confidence that God is at work in every aspect of your life—for the good. This discovery will enable you to have day-to-day power in the midst of a heavy course load, stress, and tension. It will give you greater peace while living in tight quarters with roommates. It will give you confidence to stand strong in your relationships so you won't have to hide out behind the paper fortress of courting, which is another way of saying, "I like to avoid intimacy."

Discovering the covenants brings energy to living the Christian life. It

> **Even as I type this into my computer, the spell check does not recognize "covenantal," and many of us are equally unfamiliar with the words "covenant" and "covenantal," as well as the principles. So, like Josiah, there must be a covenant revival in our lives.**

gives us the inertia to live a life of integrity while the forces of impurity are pulling at us. Most importantly, the covenant discovery helps us to know the intensity with which God works towards us for our good. It's through the covenant that He says, "I will work for you with all My heart and soul and with all My strength."

Through covenant, God becomes our partner in all of life. The four things that Josiah discovered are the same four things that we must discover in order to bring about a covenant revival among this generation so that we can Christianize the world.

> Through covenant, God becomes our partner in all of life.

1. The Definition of the Covenant

The scroll that Shaphan and Josiah found was the book of Deuteronomy. In chapter 29, verse 12, we read, "You are standing here in order to enter into a covenant with the Lord your God, a covenant the Lord is making with you this day and sealing with an oath." Covenants and oaths were familiar terms for the people of the Bible. For God to take an oath is a big deal, and God goes further: He takes on the responsibility of affirming the oath as well as the curses of the oath.

The oath is unbreakable.

I love the stories of John Grisham. There's always the scene where the lawyer calls a witness to the stand, and before the witness testifies to anything, the bailiff makes him place his hand on the Bible and promise to tell the whole truth.

That's what God is doing in verse 12 when He makes the oath. God Himself is taking the stand and places His hand on His Word. He swears by Himself to tell the whole truth and nothing but the truth so help Himself. By making an oath, God was binding Himself to the human race. **His oath becomes the guarantee of our lives.** He does this to remove our doubt and fear of trusting in Him.

The oath is unconditional.

Verse 13 of chapter 29 says, "to confirm you this day as his people, that he may be your God as he promised you and as he swore to your fathers, Abraham, Isaac and Jacob."

When God makes an oath, He breaks into our lives by making promises to love us and bless us and protect us. He swears by Himself to bring it to pass. In an oath, God is the only one who makes the covenant and keeps the covenant. In our state of spiritual anarchy God remained true to Himself for our lives. That does not, however, give us the freedom to do as we please, as we will see later on in this chapter.

An oath is unlimited.
Chapter 29:14-15 says, "I am making this covenant, with its oath, not only with you who are standing here with us today in the presence of the Lord our God but also with those who are not here today." When Josiah heard these words, it had been 850 years since they were written. So, God has extended His oath from Moses to Josiah and from generation to generation. Verses 14 and 15 reveal the scope of the covenant.

In Houston, where I speak often, a church has put up an advertisement of its services on billboards. I have to say that these are the coolest signs I have ever seen. They are blue and white—blue on the top, white on the bottom, and up in the left-hand corner it says, "Jesus Loves You." In the bottom right-hand corner it says, "No Matter What." Now that describes the definition of covenant in one simple phrase. **No matter what.**

The definition of covenant is that God voluntarily joins Himself to His creation. His covenant is unbreakable, unconditional, and unlimited no matter what. Now, that's cool.

So wherever you are now in your relationship with Him, just think that long ago, He made a promise to love you, to protect you, and to provide for you. And He has been true to you no matter what.

2. The Demands of the Covenant

Josiah's kingdom faced the same problem that Moses and Israel faced. Verse 25 says, "Because this people abandoned the covenant of the Lord, the God of their fathers, the covenant he made with them when he brought them out of Egypt." In other words, He directed His anger at them because they turned their backs on Him.

So in verse 29 we read, "The things revealed belong to us and to our children forever," which means the generations after them, including our generation. Moses, like Josiah, had to remind them of the covenant, and we today need to be reminded of the demands of the covenant.

God has designed for us a spectacular way to live, but with that life comes a great deal of responsibility. We must each know the demands of His covenantal way of life. There are four of them.

> *The definition of covenant is that God voluntarily joins Himself to His creation. His covenant is unbreakable, unconditional, and unlimited no matter what.*

The covenant says to the Lord, "It's all yours."

Look at Deuteronomy 30:2-3: "Return to the Lord your God and obey him with all your heart and with all your soul according to everything I command you today, then the Lord your God will restore your fortunes." Moses was looking ahead to see if there would be a time when Israel would be scattered. There was. The nation was dispersed in 586 B.C. and again in A.D. 70. And the message is simple: if you're scattered, then remember whose you are, where you belong, and then return to the Lord.

The enemies of the covenantal way of living in this country are pride, selfishness, status quo, and materialism.

As a result, it creates the idea of ownership—the idea that I can do whatever I want with all that I have. It doesn't really matter. Our lives begin to scatter because the more we gather to ourselves the more we realize that, under our rule, everything will fall apart. **Only then do we see that there is another Owner who is bigger than we are.** He owns everything in the world and everything that we have in our little worlds.

The challenge of covenant is that we would take everything in our lives and say, "Lord I am in covenant with You and my life is all Yours." No matter how far away selfishness, pride, and materialism may have taken you, God can bring anyone back from the furthest and coldest parts of the heart.

Every individual must choose to be in covenant.

Israel stood by the shore of the Jordan, facing Canaan and the promised land. Moses said, "Each of you must choose for yourself the covenant." All can choose! Look at the first word in verse 10 of chapter 30. It says, "If you obey the Lord." Look at the last line of that verse, "…and turn to the Lord your God with all your heart." The importance of the word "choose" is clarified again in verse 19: "Now choose life, so that you and your children may live."

This generation has approached God with a calculated cynicism. There is such a sense of despair and dismay that we withhold our decisions to move into covenant.

I am not trying to speak for everybody in my generation. I know for me cynicism has come naturally. I learned it myself as a baby lying in a crib watching that mobile twisting around, thinking, "Yep, it's coming down on me." But I embraced the covenant for myself. I understand each one of us as individuals—not as a religious group on campus, a church, or a CrossSeekers group, but as individuals—must choose to abandon ourselves for Him and embrace the covenant.

When individuals who embrace the covenant for themselves come together as a Bible study group, or a CrossSeekers group, there is power. There you have a group of individuals committed to covenant, and as a result, they begin to change the environment and culture around them.

Many times what keeps college students from moving into covenant and embracing the covenant is that they live with secret sins. You try to strike a deal with God so you can live a non-covenantal life and still have the blessings of God. But God doesn't bargain with us; there must be a complete surrender to Him. All the things we want from God cannot come into our lives through a half-hearted commitment. There must be a personal involvement, a new resolve in our heart, that we would move into a new state of belief, wholly devoted—that we would commit ourselves and embrace the covenant.

All God's relationships with man are covenantal.

God is not random. Many people have grown up believing that sometimes God is on, and when He is on He is really good, and sometimes He is off, and when He is off He is terrible. And that view makes having a relationship with God impossible.

God is very consistent when He deals with us. **He always deals with us through covenant.** We are under covenant whether we want to be or not. We get to choose how we relate to God. **We get to choose whether we know a God of blessings or a God of convictions.** God relates to us on the basis of these two categories.

God always responds covenantally to His people.

Two sides of the covenant are seen in the last line of Deuteronomy 30:16. Look at what it says: "The Lord your God will bless you." Look at the first line in verse 18: "I declare to you this day that you will certainly be destroyed." By our actions we choose how we experience God. Conviction is guaranteed when we put ourselves first, when we misuse our lives, and when we leave God out of the equation. God responds to us through

> **All God's relationships with man are covenantal.**

these circumstances. When we follow His rule and live out His will and hold fast to His Word, God relates to us through His blessings.

The reality of this is that you and I get to choose. To believe that God is random in our lives and that we have no power of choice is like blaming the inventor of the fork for being fat.

The truth is that we do have a choice as to how God relates to us on the basis of His covenant. The same covenant can be to us the covenant of blessing or the covenant of conviction. We get to choose. God monitors our lives according to how we respond to Him.

There are blessings and curses in the covenant.
Moses stands before Israel and sets out the stark contrasts of the covenant when he speaks in Deuteronomy 30:19, "I have set before you life and death, blessings and curses." There are two sides to the covenant: keep the covenant and there will be blessings; break the covenant and there will be discipline and suffering. Even in the new covenant that is still true. Follow Christ totally and there will be blessings; defy the covenant and your life will not work.

Now let's deal with each side of the covenant.

Deuteronomy 28 is divided into two parts. Verses 1-14 are the blessings of the covenant, and verses 15-68 are the curses of the covenant.

a. ***The blessings of the covenant.*** You must come to grips with the fact that God loves you and wants your life to work. The emphasis of the work of God is not just going to heaven but also bringing heaven to earth through the life that we live—that the whole blessing would rest upon us. God is looking for people who will be obedient. Even as you thank Him for His blessings, He gives you more. When we embrace the covenant for ourselves we place ourselves in a position to experience the life and love of God.

If you look back at Deuteronomy 28:2, it says that all the blessings will come upon you and overtake you. In covenant blessings, you are not the provider; God is. The system does not work for the non-believer. The system of heaven is for the people of God. When you are with God, blessings will overtake you.

b. ***The curses of the covenant.*** Don't think that all God is going to do is bless you. We want to believe that God blesses us regardless of how we are living. If you struggle because you are under attack you can stand and win, but if you struggle because of chosen disobedience, then the curses will follow. Deuteronomy 28:20 says, "The Lord"—did you hear that?—"The Lord will send on you curses, confusion and rebuke in everything you put your hand to." In verse 25 we read, "The Lord,"—there it is again—"will cause you to be defeated."

Something inside of you has rushed to your defense and said, "But that's the Old Testament. We are no longer under law; we are under grace."

Fine, but look at Hebrews 10:26-28. Read what it says: "If we deliberately keep on sinning after we have received the knowledge of the truth, no sacrifice for sins is left, but only a fearful expectation of judgment and of raging fire that will consume the enemies of God. Anyone who rejected the law of Moses died without mercy." Look at verse 29: "How much more severely do you think a man deserves to be punished who has trampled the Son of God under foot, who has treated as an unholy thing the blood of the covenant that sanctified him, and who has insulted the Spirit of grace?" In case you're wondering, that's the New Testament.

That phrase "fearful expectation of judgment" refers to discipline in the life of a believer. What should frighten us about this is that we have become so confident in God's forgiveness and so presumptuous of His grace, that we feel safe enough to do whatever we please, unwittingly placing ourselves on the curse side of the covenant.

3. The Dynasty of the Covenant

Deuteronomy 30:20 concludes by saying, "He will give you many years in the land." Now for New Testament people the word "land" is the inheritance (heaven) that we have in the will of God and the covenant of God. The verse continues: "he swore to give to your fathers." The challenge to us is that we would live in the covenant that God has made throughout history—the covenant of salvation that He promised to Abraham and fulfilled in Jesus.

Now many say that God dealt with people in different ways at different times. He interacted with Adam in one way, with Abraham in another, with Israel in another, and with Christians today in an altogether different way. But this thinking ignores the one purpose of God seen throughout Scripture—to draw people to Himself through faith in Jesus Christ. You cannot make sense of Galatians 3:8 in any other way than to accept that God has always had one covenant of salvation throughout Scripture. Paul writes, "The Scripture foresaw that God would justify the Gentiles

> **What should frighten us about this is that we have become so confident in God's forgiveness and so presumptuous of His grace, that we feel safe enough to do whatever we please, unwittingly placing ourselves on the curse side of the covenant.**

by faith, and announced the gospel in advance to Abraham: 'All nations will be blessed through you'" (Gal. 3:8).

With God's great purpose of redemption fixed firmly in our minds, let's now look at a survey of *God's salvation history*: from the first prophecy of salvation that Adam heard in the garden, to the new covenant promised in Jeremiah.

a. The promise heard by Adam—God removes sin. "And I will put enmity between you and the woman, and between your offspring and hers; he will crush your head and you will strike his heel" (Gen. 3:15).

At the moment of the fall, God lets it be known, "There will be someone who's going to come and bring salvation." At the moment that Adam and Eve sinned, and sin, destruction and death entered this world, God says, "Adam's seed will have the victory."

God promises a rescue from the snake and his ways: we will be rescued from our sins, scars, and screw-ups. God promises to make a way for us to break out of the traps of life.

b. The covenant of David—He reigns with authority. "When your days are over and you rest with your fathers, I will raise up your offspring to succeed you, who will come from your own body, and I will establish his kingdom. He is the one who will build a house for my Name, and I will establish the throne of his kingdom forever" (2 Sam. 7:12-13).

> David's kingdom did not rest on his own strength or talent, but on God's faithfulness to all that He had promised him.

David's kingdom did not rest on his own strength or talent, but on God's faithfulness to all that He had promised him. And David sees the establishment of his son's kingdom as part of God's plan to build His house.

c. The covenant of Jeremiah—He redeems nations. "'This is the covenant I will make with the house of Israel after that time,' declares the Lord. 'I will put my law in their minds and write it on their hearts. I will be their God and they will be my people. I will forgive their wickedness and will remember their sins no more'" (Jer. 31:33,34b).

To be intimately involved with God is how His will is accomplished. The spirit of God lives inside us: guiding, directing, and counseling.

4. The Decision of the Covenant

Deuteronomy 30:14 says, "No, the word is very near you; it is in your mouth and in your heart so you may obey it." To say that it is in your mouth means that you can repeat it; you can recite it; you can understand it with your mind. To say that it is in your heart means that you can react to it with your whole person. God has placed it within you to say yes to the covenant and to live obediently under His covenant rule. Being in a covenantal relationship with God works to your advantage. **The greatest thing that you can do is to embrace it with your whole life.**

Encourage Your Group: Actions for Group Study

1. Discuss what one word summarizes the definition of "covenant" given in this chapter.
2. Discuss: Does God's faithfulness to the covenant mean that you can be sure that if God wants you to have the covenant's blessings, you are sure to get them, or does it mean that if you walk in the covenant, God is sure to give them to you?
3. Share why it is important for each person to embrace the covenant himself.

Between You and God

1. Having read this chapter, are you in covenant with God?
2. How do the covenants help you to know what is in the heart of God?
3. Think of your life's greatest loves (talents, possessions, opportunities). Share with God how they flow out of God's covenant faithfulness.
4. Of all the promises of God that we've talked about in this chapter, share with God which one spoke to you most powerfully.

Just One Thing: The Single Plan of History

Just One Thing: The Single Plan of History

Chris Tomlin is a good friend of mine and a fabulous worship leader. He and I were doing a weekly Bible study in a place called Woodlands, Texas—a very affluent community where there are two classes of people: the haves and the have, have, haves. We had just finished the Bible study that night and gone out to eat. I was telling him that the week earlier I had done a conference with another worship leader who basically worshiped himself and was too "spiritual" to benefit anybody. This guy had the most amazing ability—he was able to lead worship while patting himself on the back at the same time. This doesn't make for effective ministry, but it's amazing to watch. This guy told me that 90 percent of worship is silence. So he refused to play any music that was loud, fast, positive, or energetic.

What does Revelation 5 say about why we praise God? We praise Him because of His reign. And when we stand in a place and give Him glory and honor and majesty and riches and wisdom and honor and might, we do those things because of a book. The book is not the Bible; it's not the book of Revelation. It is a book within a book. Revelation 5 is about the book of the covenant. It's the scroll of the covenant.

"Then I saw in the right hand of him who sat on the throne a scroll with writing on both sides and sealed with seven seals" (Rev. 5:1).

So as we worship, it helps to know these things. We worship Jesus because of who He is and what He has done. Revelation 5:5 says that He alone was the only one worthy to open and fulfill the new covenant. *How was it that Jesus fulfilled that new covenant?* That's what this chapter is about.

The Contents of the Covenant Book

Verse 1 says that this book was sealed with seven different seals. Seven different witnesses would always seal a will and a testament in that day and age. There would always be seven different people who would attest to it. It also says that it was written on the front and the back, which means that it contained two separate messages: it contained the message of salvation, and it contained the message of judgment.

This was the nature and the style of a covenant. This book that has the seven seals on it in Revelation 5:1 is the new covenant. We know that because the old covenant prophets present it in just the same form (Jer. 31:31; Isa. 29:11; Ezek. 1:3-10; Dan. 12:4).

Jesus established this new covenant: He would judge the earth and He would bring salvation as He rules the earth through the covenant.

The Completion of the Covenant Book

"And I saw a mighty angel proclaiming in a loud voice, 'Who is worthy to break the seals and open the scroll?' But no one in heaven or on earth or under the earth could open the scroll or even look inside it" (Rev. 5:2-3).

These verses say that God was looking to make a covenant and that no one was worthy to open the book: not Moses, not Abraham—none of the patriarchs. No one was worthy to open the book. But then Christ came as a conqueror to open up the book. How could He do that? The answer is spelled out in the remaining verses of Revelation 5.

One of the things that has happened to us as Christians in this country is that we've become gospel-hardened. The proof of that is when you hear people talk about Bible study and about the Word of God, they often use phrases like "I need something deep. I need to be in the deep things of God." When they hear somebody talk about the gospel or they hear somebody talk about the cross they say, "Yeah, yeah, yeah. I've got it. I want something deeper than that."

But it was this simple message, the message of the gospel, which changed the face of the world. It was this simple message that the disciples and the apostles used to turn cities upside down. It was with this simple message that the apostle Paul literally began building the church throughout the world. It was this simple message that Paul used to win other people to Christ. It was this single message that built the New Testament church. When you look at it in its fullness, this is as deep as it gets.

JESUS FULFILLS THE NEW COVENANT IN THREE WAYS:

A. *Through the Eminence of His Person*

"Then one of the elders said to me, 'Do not weep! See…'" (Rev. 5:5).

The Single Plan

We've got to understand in our generation that Christianity did not begin with us. Our generation is not the first to discover Christianity. Since the beginning of time God has been doing one thing. We have the tendency to believe that God did something in the Old Testament with a certain group of people, but it didn't work out. It all fell apart. We think that He had to come up with something else, and during those 400 years of silence He was thinking and mowing it over. The New Testament begins, and we think it's God's Plan B. That's not true at all! What God has been doing since the garden, He's been doing up until now.

This is what you and I have to see: **Jesus is the single plan of history.** Jesus is the single strategy of Scripture. How do we know that?

From the beginning of time God started to build a road. Since that moment He's built that road all the way down through history. Think of it in another way: since the beginning of the world God has been drawing a line. He has drawn that line through all of time, through all of history, through all of the Old Testament and through all of the New Testament. He has drawn that line up to you and to me today.

When you see this covenantal perspective of the gospel it will totally help you understand what you're carrying. It will help you understand what incredible power you're carrying on the inside of you because of the gospel. So how do we see this covenantal perspective through Scripture? By looking at Jesus as the fulfillment of the promised seed, we see that God's plan through history has always been Jesus Christ.

There are four seeds seen throughout Scripture.

1. As the Seed of Adam, Jesus brings salvation.
The first seed is found in Genesis 3. It is the prophesy that the Seed is going to come and that He is going to deal with the devil.

"And I will put enmity between you and the woman, and between your seed and her seed; he shall bruise you on the head, and you shall bruise him on the heel" (Gen. 3:15, NASB).

Where is this talked about in the New Testament?

"Since the children have flesh and blood, he too shared in their humanity so that by his death he might destroy him who holds the power of death—that is, the devil—and free those who all their lives were held in slavery by their fear of death" (Heb. 2:14).

So what's happening? God in the garden promises to destroy the devil and his works. At the right time in history Jesus comes into this world,

> We've got to understand in our generation that Christianity did not begin with us. Our generation is not the first to discover Christianity. Since the beginning of time God has been doing one thing. We have the tendency to believe that God did something in the Old Testament with a certain group of people, but it didn't work out. It all fell apart. We think that He had to come up with something else, and during those 400 years of silence He was thinking and mowing it over. The New Testament begins, and we think it's God's Plan B. That's not true at all! What God has been doing since the garden, He's been doing up until now.

places His life on the cross, and fulfills that promise. Jesus, the Seed of God, comes and renders Satan powerless, and He sets us free from everything that the enemy has done in our lives.

The story of sin and salvation is the story of two men. One lived in disobedience to God's instruction, not trusting in His goodness. The other lived in perfect obedience—a king playing a servant's role. Because of the one's disobedience, we are born separated from God. If we trust in the other's obedience, we are brought into relationship with God. The first man is Adam, the natural father of us all. The second man is Christ, who gives us access to the Father, the God of all creation, if we put our trust in Him.

2. As the Seed of Abraham, He brings success.

"I will establish my covenant as an everlasting covenant between me and you and your descendants after you for the generations to come, to be your God and the God of your descendants after you" (Gen. 17:7).

Where is that talked about in the New Testament? Where do we see that come about?

"The promises were spoken to Abraham and to his seed. The Scripture does not say 'and to seeds,' meaning many people, but 'and to your seed,' meaning one person, who is Christ" (Gal. 3:16).

So who's the seed of Abraham? Jesus is. Jesus is the Seed of Abraham. If that's true, then all of the promises made to Abraham came true in Jesus.

Jesus turbocharges the covenants. Everything that God promised in the covenants was made real in Jesus.

3. As the Seed of David, He brings strength.

"The Lord has sworn to David, a truth from which he will not turn back; 'Of the fruit of your body I will set upon your throne'" (Ps. 132:11, NASB).

When He says "the fruit of your body" he's talking about the seed of his body. Where is that seen in the New Testament?

"But he was a prophet and knew that God had promised him on oath that he would place one of his descendants on his throne. Seeing what was ahead, he spoke of the resurrection of the Christ, that he was not abandoned to the grave, nor did his body see decay. God has raised this Jesus to life, and we are all witnesses of the fact. Exalted to the right hand of

> *Jesus turbocharges the covenants. Everything that God promised in the covenants was made real in Jesus.*

God, he has received from the Father the promised Holy Spirit and has poured out what you now see and hear" (Acts 2:30-33).

It was not David who ascended into heaven, but Christ. Why is David speaking of the resurrection? Because he looked forward and saw Jesus beating death. What happened at the resurrection is that Jesus ascended up to the Father and received His kingdom.

4. As the Seed of Jeremiah, He brings His Spirit.
"'The time is coming,' declares the Lord, 'when I will make a new covenant with the house of Israel and with the house of Judah. This is the covenant I will make with the house of Israel after that time,' declares the Lord. 'I will put my law in their minds and write it on their hearts. I will be their God, and they will be my people. No longer will a man teach his neighbor, or a man his brother, saying, 'Know the Lord,' because they will all know me, from the least of them to the greatest,' declares the Lord. 'For I will forgive their wickedness and will remember their sins no more'" (Jer. 31:31,33-34).

Where is this new covenant talked about in the New Testament?

"When Christ came as high priest of the good things that are already here, he went through the greater and more perfect tabernacle that is not man-made, that is to say, not a part of this creation. He did not enter by means of the blood of goats and calves; but he entered the Most Holy Place once for all by his own blood, having obtained eternal redemption" (Heb. 9:11-12).

God in the new covenant to Jeremiah promises to bring full salvation, the presence of the Holy Spirit living on the inside of us, and the blessing of God. At the right time Jesus came into this world, lived a perfect life, and died on the cross. The Holy Spirit makes those things a reality in our lives. When you look at this throughout Scripture what you see is that Jesus is the single plan of God. Jesus is the single plan in Scripture. God has been drawing a line of redemption all the way through the Old Testament, all the way through the New Testament, and then also right up into our lives.

When you look at the covenants and you look at Jesus as the Seed and the single plan in Scripture, it is clear that He is the Son of God. You see that He is eminently qualified to fulfill the new covenant.

Remember the eminence of His presence. Following is the second way Jesus fulfills the new covenant.

B. *Through His Essential Performance*

"He came and took the scroll from the right hand of Him who sat on the throne" (Rev. 5:7).

How Jesus took the book is His performance. How Jesus took the covenant was through what He did. Revelation 5 lists the three ways that Jesus performs.

1. As a Lion, He defends.

"'See, the Lion of the tribe of Judah…'" (Rev. 5:5b).

That He performs as a lion means that He is a defender and a judge. As the Lion, He judges the sin in man's life. This is the picture of a king ruling from his throne, like a lion.

2. As a Lamb, He delivers.

"I saw a Lamb, looking as if it had been slain, standing…" (Rev. 5:6).

As the Lamb, He is the salvation of our lives. As the Lamb, He gathers us to Himself. As the Lamb, He is the Lover, the Counselor, the Blesser, the Healer, the Giver, and our new start. The Lamb has experienced everything that you and I have experienced. He has touched and endured everything that you and I have endured. As the Lamb, He feels our struggles and our sorrows and has experienced them for Himself. As the Lamb, He hung on the cross in our place. The cross was not God's second best. Christ was God's sacrifice prepared before the foundations of the world. Think about it! Believe it!

3. As Lord, He directs.

"He came and took the scroll from the right hand of him who sat on the throne" (Rev. 5:7).

As the Lord we see Him as the Ruler and Director of our lives. The resurrection is proof that Jesus can walk up and take the book out of the hand of God. Jesus is the Ruler and the Lord. Not only does Jesus rule over the earth but He also rules in our lives if we choose to let Him be that Director.

Seeing what He's done as the Director, the Deliverer, and the Defender should affect the way we live.

Jesus is the single plan of Scripture; He's the single plan of God. All that God promised in the Old Testament was fulfilled in the New Testament.

When we put our faith in it, it becomes real in us. When you look at all that was promised and how He fulfilled it, you will not only see Jesus as the promised Seed but also as the living Son. When you see Him as the Son, you see His performance.

Flashback! Jesus fulfills the new covenant in three ways:
A. Through the eminence of His person
B. Through His essential performance

And now we see that He fulfills it:

C. Through His Exalted Position
"Then I looked and heard the voice of many angels, numbering thousands upon thousands, and ten thousand times ten thousand. They encircled the throne and the living creatures and the elders. In a loud voice they sang: 'Worthy is the Lamb, who was slain, to receive power and wealth and wisdom and strength and honor and glory and praise!' Then I heard every creature in heaven and on earth and under the earth and on the sea, and all that is in them, singing: 'To him who sits on the throne [His exalted position] and to the Lamb [who hung in our place], be praise and honor and glory and power, for ever and ever!'" (Rev. 5:11-13).

When we worship, we see Him in His exalted position. We see Him as He is. We see Him the way Isaiah saw Him in chapter 6 when he said, "I saw the Lord seated on a throne, high and exalted, and the train of his robe filled the temple" (Isa. 6:1). When we worship and when we sing, we see Jesus as He rightly is. We see Him as the One who reigns over all the earth.

The Community of the New Covenant Book

In Revelation chapter 5 he talks about the community:
"You have made them to be a kingdom and priests to serve our God, and they will reign on the earth" (Rev. 5:10).

He's talking about us! That's you and me. Here's an example of how God uses us to Christianize and transform the world, one life at a time:

My best friend in the whole world lives in Oklahoma City. Every time I'm there, we go to a little Mexican restaurant for dinner. There's a waitress there who waits on us every time we go. One day last year, she came over to our table and said, "I just got engaged!" While we were admiring her ring, she said, "He just got out of prison." Red flags started popping up in my mind. "Bing! Bing!" She continued, "He's just recovering from a drug addiction." "Bing! Bing!" **"He's not really a Christian, but he's a good man."** "Bing! Bing! Bing!" All of these red flags were just flying up in front of my face—I felt like a bull. I didn't know her well enough to say, "That's a horrible idea," so I mumbled, "Well, I'd be interested to find out what happens later on."

We went in again some time later. This time she said, "Someone told me one time that in order to be a Christian that you couldn't just check it off but that you had to go through something. Do you know what I'm talking about?" I said, "Yes I do." I had this little book called *How to Make Life All Good*. It's basically a gospel outline. I pointed to a picture of a man on the left side of the outline and said, "We enter this world separated from God. We try whatever we can do to get into the presence of God. We try to be good. Do you ever try to be good?" "Yeah." "We try to go to church. Do you go to church?" "Yeah." "Ever tried to clean your life up, getting rid of the things you think God might not approve of?" "Yeah." I said, "Everything we try to do comes up just short of where God is. It lands in the valley of good intentions."

Now as I walked her through the little book, she would laugh at me—and believe me, I wasn't telling any jokes. I thought, "This is going to be tough." Then I said, "At just the right time in history, Jesus came to die on the cross. That cross became like a bridge. With one hand He was reaching out to God over to heaven, and with the other hand He was reaching out to the world. To anyone who would believe that Jesus died for sin and came back to life, the Bible says to that person, you get to have all your sins erased. You are forgiven, and when you die, you get to miss hell and make heaven. Does that make sense?"

Just as I said, "Does that make sense?" she dashed off to wait on tables—taking orders, delivering food, and refilling drinks.

She returned and said, "Okay, go ahead." I said, "I know you sort of well. I know enough about your dating life that I would say you're probably still on the left-hand side of the page." She said, "Yeah, my deal is control. I want to control everything. I want to control my life. I realize I can't do it. I think that I need Christ." I went, "Cha Ching!" I held up my hand and she gave me a high-five. I said, "That's it! You just answered your question! You can't do your life by yourself. You can't control your life by yourself." I finished the rest of the little book. "You put your faith in Jesus in what He did on the cross. You move from being separated from God into the presence of God. He comes to live in you." **I said, "You know I wouldn't have told you any of this if you wouldn't have asked me."** She said, "I know." I said, "The Bible says the way that all of this becomes real is that you've got to ask Him. Romans 10:13 says, 'Whoever will call on the name of the Lord will be saved.' The word *saved* means you get to start over. If you'd be willing, I'd like to help you ask Him to come into your life. Would you be willing to let me lead you in a simple prayer?" And she said, "Yes, I'd love that."

So this woman sat down at my table in the middle of this Mexican restaurant and gave her life to Christ! I do this for a living, but I'm telling you that, to my amazement, this woman prayed through this simple prayer: "God, I believe You are the Son of God. I believe You died for me. I know my sins separated me from You, and I believe that You're real and that You are the One." She prayed it right through, line by line. "And tonight I ask You to come into my life." **I looked up, and this girl was weeping in the middle of the restaurant.** My best friend was weeping. Do you know why that happened? It's because Jesus is the Son of God, and with His presence comes power.

She said, "I feel like a thousand pounds have been lifted off of me." I said, "Do you know what you're feeling? Forgiveness." She said, "It's real, isn't it?" I said, "Yeah." The power of God was at our table that night. The power of God landed on that woman. That little story has power because the promises that God made He kept in Jesus. Jesus is the only door into the presence of God.

What happened to her that night, at that table, in that little Mexican restaurant was that God drew a single line of redemption throughout all of history. He drew it from the Old Testament with the patriarchs and prophets, through to the New Testament with the person of Jesus, and to my local Mexican restaurant to that young girl's life.

This is true for every one of us. What Jesus did by fulfilling all those covenants on the cross and by taking those promises to a higher level, He does in every one of us. If you don't have this type of relationship with Christ, can you offer up the same prayer as the young waitress and be ready for Christ to do a miracle in your life?

The Chorus of the New Covenant Book
"In a loud voice they sang: 'Worthy is the Lamb, who was slain, to receive power and wealth and wisdom and strength and honor and

> **Lord Jesus,**
>
> **Thank You for being the Covenant Keeper. You have fulfilled every promise of God as the single plan of history. All that You have and are You have given me.**
>
> **You have shown Your good motives to me through the covenant, and You are the guarantee of my life. I embrace who You have declared me to be, and I willingly place my life in covenant with You.**

glory and praise!' Then I heard every creature in heaven and on earth and under the earth and on the sea, and all that is in them, singing: 'To him who sits on the throne and to the Lamb be praise and honor and glory and power, for ever and ever!'" (Rev. 5:12-13).

This is about you and me. It's about you singing. We have to quit reading this chapter like it's about some other group that is going to do it for us. That's not true. When we worship we're saying, "God, this is my life." We cannot honor Jesus in some pretend way. We can't pretend like we do it. He receives honor through how we live our lives—through covenantal living. **Our greatest act of worship is to live by His covenants and through His covenants.** He's worthy of our dreams. He's worthy of our desires and our destiny.

The chorus of worship is not something that you just sing in the middle of a song; it's not just reserved for an evening time; it's not something that happens before the speaker gets up to speak. To say that life is worship is to say that you've chosen to place your life in covenant and that because of who Jesus is and what He's done—He's fulfilled uniquely the book of the covenant—our response is that we would live out these six principles of the CrossSeekers covenant.

Encourage Your Group: Actions for Group Study

1. In Revelation 5, we see that the Lamb is the only one worthy to open the scroll. Jesus alone fulfilled the covenant. Now, share with one another how viewing this covenantal aspect of salvation helps you answer the claim that salvation can be found in someone other than Jesus.
2. Think about what your job description on the basis of the new covenant is to be. Be prepared to share your answers with the group.
3. Write down in the margin your answer to "Why is the gospel so powerful?"

Between You and God

1. Pray with God to help you know for sure the single plan of history.
2. Think about how God's faithfulness to the covenants heightens your sensitivity to the depth and beauty of the Christian life. In a prayerful spirit, talk to God about these.

In the next six chapters, we will move from looking at Jesus as the Author and Finisher of the Covenant to looking at specific areas of our lives where we can live covenantally. In preparation for the rest of the book, please look at the following verses, their contexts, and how they relate to the definition of the CrossSeekers values given below.

Write it in your own words here.

Value	Definition	Verses	Your Words
INTEGRITY	Not what you do but who you are.	Hebrews 13:20-21 Proverbs 11:3 Titus 3:3-5	
SPIRITUAL GROWTH	A privilege given to us at the new birth.	John 16:13 1 Corinthians 2:9-13 Philippians 3:13-14	
WITNESS	Provoking others to Christ with the blessings of God on our lives.	3 John 2 Psalm 35:21 Psalm 122:7 Acts 22:15	
SERVICE	Building God's house	1 Timothy 1:12 2 Timothy 2:2 2 Timothy 4:17-18 Ephesians 2:10	
PURITY	Conforming your life to the will of God.	Ephesians 1:4 Titus 2:14 2 Timothy 2:21	
CHRISTLIKE RELATIONSHIPS	Supporting the prerogative of God.	Proverbs 17:9 Luke 6:32-35 Proverbs 18:24	

SESSION 2

The Truth Behind Performance: The Life of Integrity

The Challenge
Transforming the World Through Covenant Living

The Truth Behind Performance: The Life of Integrity

We live in a world that has a TV show called "The Real World," when it's about the most pathetically fake thing there is. Seven beautiful people live in luxury, rent-free. Does this sound like your real world? They even have auditions for this show—can you believe it?—auditions! These people are so busy playing to the cameras that they do not have time to be real. But people watch it. And why? We don't care. Integrity has disappeared from our national landscape.

Integrity has been replaced with tolerance and its twin, political correctness. The mindset of political correctness sees God as the guy guarding the velvet rope outside of the elite club everyone wants to get into. Political correctness is the new way of kissing up to God, so that He will like us and give us a better seat at the dessert table.

For those of you out of the loop, I provide, below, a list of words and their politically correct (PC) counterparts.

A Sample English to PC Glossary

Smart	is	cerebrally advantaged
Hunting	is	stalking non-humans
Ugly	is	visually inconvenienced
Liar	is	reality stylist
Gossip	is	issuing a misstatement
Dead	is	really late for work
Adultery	is	1. progressively minded marriage
		2. user friendly
Mean	is	kindness impaired
Racist	is	colorless thinking
Lost	is	unchurched
Sin	is	adult entertainment
Hell	is	a temperature intensive location

Let's see if you can translate this sentence. "When the unchurched, visually inconvenienced reality stylist is really late for work, we can know that he is paying for his adult entertainment in a temperature intensive location forever." *(Answer: When the lost, ugly liar dies, he'll pay for his sin in hell forever.)*

With a society so touchy about how things are said, we all have to use our eyeteeth to watch what we are saying. Speaking and not offending anyone is difficult at best and sometimes nearly impossible.

What happens when PC finds its way into the church? The Bible will be referred to as "the processed tree carcass of celestial information."

Scriptures would read differently:

Genesis: Their eyes were opened and they were both in a state of clothing optional lifestyle.

Exodus: It was an ecologically sound idea for God to put the ten suggestions on stone, because it saved paper and affirmed the life of trees.

Numbers 13: We saw it, and it is a land that flows with high protein by-product stolen from voiceless, defenseless bovine companions and high energy, high calorie nectar unjustly appropriated from innocent but hardly defenseless buzzing insects.

And more:

"Oh you of a vertically disadvantaged faith."
"Money is the root of all behavioral divergence."
"The harvest is plentiful, but the workers have been downsized."
"Visually inhibited leading the visually inhibited."
"Let him who is ethically unchallenged cast the first writing tablet."

PC is nothing more than a blind adherence to what is acceptable. Let's not forget that in our recent history the last society to be considered PC killed millions of Jews.

As if that was not reason enough, the problem with PC is that it is completely external. It has nothing to do with the inner state of our lives. PC has enabled people to display goodness without having to be a good person. It's all style and no substance.

It was precisely this type of society that Jeremiah found himself living in. It was a society of rules, regulations, and religion without reason.

> PC has enabled people to display goodness without having to be a good person. It's all style and no substance.

The Challenge
Transforming the World Through Covenant Living

These things did not get into the people's hearts. **It was obedience through sheer will power. It was performance without personal involvement.**

If ever there was a generation of politically correct followers of God, it was in the days of Jeremiah. The religious show was going on, but the nation was in crisis. The people had drifted far from their former obedience to the God of Abraham. Lawlessness and sin filled the city of Jerusalem. Though the sacrifices continued in the temple, Jehovah was not revered, much less truly worshiped. Personal integrity was based on external behavior. Rules and regulations were the order of the day.

This was an awesome opportunity for a prophet of God.

Identifies the Covenant in our Being

A covenant biography
Jeremiah was strikingly handsome. Reared in a tiny town outside of Jerusalem as the son of a priest, he had grown up loving the temple, the traditions, the people, and the God of Abraham and Moses. On one trip to Jerusalem the test of integrity came for Jeremiah, and his entire life was radically changed.

He had made the one-hour walk from his home to Jerusalem many times. However, this walk would be different. This time his destiny would be laid out before him. This time he would meet God. Standing outside the city, overlooking its magnificence, enjoying the sounds, the energy that brought life to the giant walls, Jeremiah heard God: "…I appointed you as a prophet to the nations" (Jer. 1:5).

The dream of every young Jewish man was to meet God personally and, like Moses, speak with God. Much more, to be the prophet and speak for God to the nation—that was the ultimate. The idea of knowing God so closely and being allowed to represent His desires and demands was the greatest challenge and the most overwhelming honor any Jewish man could receive. Yet, despite the awesome requirements of the office, and the scores of other young men He could have wanted, God specifically chose Jeremiah and without hesitation declared his destiny: he'd be a prophet.

For Jeremiah to accept the role of the prophet during this critical time

> He took care to help the young prophet to prepare him to succeed. God did so by presenting to Jeremiah the single basis for integrity: "Before I formed you in the womb I knew you, before you were born I set you apart" (Jer. 1:5).

would forever seal his uniqueness and unleash his greatness. Yet, his initial response was not one of excitement and confidence. Instead he muttered, "I do not know how to speak; I am only a child" (Jer. 1:6).

How could this remarkable young man who would ultimately possess such prophetic boldness, such power, courage, and tenacity respond to the discovery of his destiny in such a dismally negative way? Jeremiah's struggle was that he thought integrity was something you do. So if God was calling him to be a prophet, he would need to be able to perform as a speaker. But God took time to deal with him and reshaped the way Jeremiah perceived integrity. He showed him that integrity is not about what you do—it's who you are. And if God calls you to be a prophet, then He will empower you to do all that a prophet does. The gentleness of God in helping Jeremiah was awesome. I would have loved to have been there!

I can see Jeremiah stopping to enjoy the view of the city. After all, Jerusalem was the center of his world, and for him at least, the most important city on earth. Everything he loved was there. The men he honored and the traditions he adored dominated this city of David. As Jeremiah stood gazing upon Jerusalem, thousands of years of history stared him in the face. For this remarkable young man with so much potential, this was the defining event of his life. Even though he was a student of the prophets and Hebrew custom, nothing could have prepared him for the encounter that was about to take place.

At that moment, that powerful moment, God spoke gently and personally.

It is obvious that God recognized Jeremiah's struggle with a true understanding of real integrity and that He took care to help the young prophet to prepare him to succeed. God did so by presenting to Jeremiah the single basis for integrity: "Before I formed you in the womb I knew you, before you were born I set you apart" (Jer. 1:5).

God said, in so many words, "Jeremiah, the way I see you and the way I want you to see your ability to walk in complete integrity is not based upon the power you possess, or the office you hold, or the fortune you have amassed, or even because people hold you in a place of honor. Who you are—your worth and intrinsic value—comes from Me. I have the right to place demands upon your life, and your integrity is based upon your acceptance of those demands and allowing My will to be fulfilled. Integrity is not about doing righteous deeds or refusing to do unrighteous deeds. It is about you accepting My right to lead your life to complete My purpose."

"Long before I created you in your mother's womb I designed a destiny so valuable, so powerful, and so successful for you. My ideas concerning you proceeded the creation of the world. I knew who you would be. I planned everything about you. I determined your race, your size, your sex, and your personality. I consecrated you with divine purpose. You are great because I placed value and purpose on you. Now, it is critically important that you see what I see in you and imagine what I have imagined about you, and fully receive it. Now that's genuine integrity!"

God demanded that Jeremiah understand that his self-worth, and therefore his self-esteem, his self-identity, and his self-image all came from God. What God said about Jeremiah was the truth—not Jeremiah's beliefs, thoughts, emotions, reasoning, or his life experiences. Regardless of the verdict laid down by parents, friends, heroes, or enemies, what God declared determined Jeremiah's worth and abilities. His fulfillment of God's verdict determined his integrity!

Jeremiah Introduced the New Covenant with Boldness

Like millions of people today, Jeremiah saw integrity as simply keeping the law and following the religious leaders and their regulations—not specifically following the demands and challenges God was placing on him. *He believed that actions and attitudes revealed the content of one's life.* Isn't this what we do many times today? We make integrity an issue of how we act. We must quit making integrity an external thing. If we don't, we will remain in a state of perpetual failure. As long as we define ourselves solely by our actions we will never be able to deal with the hurts of our lives, confess the needs of our lives, and admit to the failures of our lives. We have a desperate need to be honest with ourselves, both about who we are and about who God made us to be.

Jeremiah failed to understand that the question of integrity was not whether or not he would go to the temple to make a sacrifice, but it was, "Would he be a prophet—would he obey?"

> You are great because I placed value and purpose on you. Now, it is critically important that you see what I see in you and imagine what I have imagined about you, and fully receive it.

> Will you be a prophet? This is the central question of covenantal integrity. To do so, you must stand up and stand out of the culture. You can no longer define yourself by your behavior, but rather by who you are. And who are you?

Will you be a prophet? This is the central question of covenantal integrity. To do so, you must stand up and stand out of the culture. You can no longer define yourself by your behavior, but rather by who you are. And who are you?

Jeremiah was so caught up in the religious culture of his moment, (thinking that pleasing God was fulfilling a religious rule) that he could not respond correctly to God. This is where many of us are. What God was teaching Jeremiah then is what He is teaching us today. Quit identifying yourself by your behavior, your drive, and your sin. Who you are is not what you do. Find out who you are and what you do will follow. When we do what we do because of the way we perceive ourselves, integrity happens.

This critical moment was a foreshadowing of the ultimate prophetic moment of Jeremiah's life. He was to be a prophet to the nations—not just Israel. He would introduce the new covenant and with it the basis for true integrity. Just as Jeremiah had to come to a personal experience of receiving the will of God and fully walking it out, so would every believer who would follow. God spoke through the prophet, "I will put my law in their minds and write it on their hearts. I will be their God, and they will be my people" (Jer. 31:33).

Jeremiah had seen an entirely new world. God would never again be served by religious traditions. True integrity would never again be external, but internal. It would never again be about rules or religious regulations; it would be about God writing His own will on the hearts of individuals and their willingness to obey.

Much of our frustration today is based on our attempt to find true integrity based on religious actions. No wonder we have lost integrity!

Jesus Inaugurated the New Covenant with His Blood

Ultimately it would be Jesus—not Jeremiah—who would inaugurate the new covenant and its powerful integrity.

That night when the disciples entered the upper room with Jesus, the table was already set for the final supper. The table was curved, so as each climbed around the table they could see each other.

Having given the bread, Jesus took the cup and lifted it so that it was the central focus for everyone in the room. Christ said, "This is my blood of the covenant, which is poured out for many for the forgiveness of sins" (Matt. 26:28). Though at the time the disciples may not have understood what was ahead, they were painfully aware of what blood covenant meant.

It was part of their heritage, and having seen it and having been taught about it, blood covenant in their minds was a heifer, a goat, or a ram with its neck sliced on either side. The knife was driven into the breastbone with a downward motion so that the bone would crack. The flesh would tear open, and the carcass would fall into two separate pieces across from each other to form a pathway in between. Jesus, that night, had marked Himself as the ultimate sacrifice. He would remove sin and the punishment we deserve for our sin, once and for all.

The promise in the Old Testament is made true in the New: the death of Jesus for our sins is the foundation of the new covenant. When Jerusalem was leveled in A.D. 70, it was further testimony that the coming of Jesus was in fact the ending of the old covenant and the beginning of the new. There was the replacement of shadows with reality—Jesus Christ Himself.

For this reason, Jesus, at the Last Supper, spoke of "the new covenant in my blood" (Luke 22:20).

God the Father and God the Son had made a covenant to redeem the lives of the human race. The Spirit of God would bring this covenant of rescue to people from all the nations.

"In the same way, after the supper he took the cup, saying, 'This cup is the new covenant in my blood, which is poured out for you'" (Luke 22:20).

Everything Jeremiah had seen, Jesus fulfilled! Through the powerful blood of Jesus an entirely new way to God was established. The Holy Spirit had been poured out in the new covenant, and people could know God in a personal and powerful way!

So integrity is not an issue of the law—what we do. Integrity is an issue of covenant. Integrity flows from the heart of each newborn believer. As born again, new covenant people, we can be real people in the real world while still living lives that glorify God. Integrity flows

> **Look at Hebrews 7:27-28; 9:28, and 10:11-12.**
> 1. What do these verses say about the blood of Christ?_____
> 2. How do these verses demonstrate the supremacy of Christ as both Priest and Sacrifice?_____
> 3. Why does the death of Jesus secure atonement for all of eternity?_____

> *So integrity is not an issue of the law—what we do. Integrity is an issue of covenant. Integrity flows from the heart of each newborn believer.*

out of who we are—sons of God!

Jesus was proclaiming, as forcefully as possible, that a whole new way was opening up. This fabulous new way was not to be blocked by going back and trying to live Christianity by viewing integrity as an outward performance. The Lord insisted, "Neither do men pour new wine into old wineskins. If they do, the skins will burst, the wine will run out and the wineskins will be ruined. No, they pour new wine into new wineskins, and both are preserved" (Matt. 9:17).

Paul Illustrates the Covenant in the Life of the Believer

In his love for Jesus, the apostle Paul played the role of evangelist, preacher, administrator, theologian, and apologist. He had the task of defending the new covenant teaching of Jesus. It was not easy. Paul harnessed all of his knowledge of Scripture to defend the claim that an individual can receive the covenant of salvation. To do so, Paul returned to the one to whom the covenant had been given—Abraham. In passages such as Galatians 3, Paul argues that Abraham believed the good news about Jesus and that the covenant of salvation has always been based on faith, not works. Unfortunately, this view remains a radical idea for many Christians today! Having believed in salvation by faith alone, we think we make ourselves better on our own effort, without God's help. This is foolishness.

Christians—a threatening people

Let's set the stage by seeing how the author of Hebrews understood Jesus' words at the last supper: "By calling this covenant 'new,' he has made the first one obsolete; and what is obsolete and aging will soon disappear" (Heb. 8:13). What was he thinking? Was the old covenant "ready to disappear"? For those whose whole way of life was defined by the old covenant, this disappearance threatened their very lives. After all, many saw the old covenant as what defined their relationship to God—and to each other.

God had been at work since Abraham, calling, preserving, judging, forgiving and blessing His people Israel. Through Moses, God had given the people an elaborate system of sacrifices, feasts, and rituals to distinguish the nation and people of Israel.

Christianity threatened the Jewish way of life.

Christians claimed that Jesus had come as the Messiah, and many in

Israel rejected this claim. After all, their rejection of the messenger had resulted in the crucifixion of Jesus. Their rejection of the message naturally led to the persecution of the early Christians. The Christian claims raised a huge question for the Jewish people as a whole. How could they respond to this threat?

Stephen was an irresistible witness. He spoke against Jerusalem and the Law. Those in power understood that Christianity threatened both the existence of the temple and their understanding of the Old Testament. They had reason to be afraid of the early Christians. After all, they wanted to Christianize and transform the world. The early Christians were a meek and peaceful band who would rather die than live by the sword. Nevertheless, at the very heart of their faith was the implicit end of the old covenant. The threat of Christianity was not from a holy war of Christian antagonism. The threat was God Himself—by raising Jesus from the dead, God proved that Christ fulfilled the old covenant.

> They had reason to be afraid of the early Christians. After all, they wanted to Christianize and transform the world.

God had promised that He would write His will on their hearts, be their God, and cause them to know Him personally. He would be merciful to their iniquities and remember their sins no more.

When Jerusalem fell to the Romans in A.D. 70, and the temple was destroyed, no longer could sacrifices be made in Judaism. The Levitical priesthood came to an end. But that should not trouble us; decades before, at just the right time, Jesus, our Lamb, died for us. Even if we wanted to sacrifice a sin offering, we couldn't—the temple is not there—but God be praised that we don't have to.

> As a Christian student, you are responsible to God and God alone for your integrity.

If we still think that we must do something to gain favor before God, we are acting in foolishness. Yet the church of Jesus Christ is still filled with those who want to hold on to a legalistic way of thinking. Stop it!

In Paul's day, this thinking consumed members of the church at Rome. They insisted upon keeping integrity as an outward idea. As a result, they were busy judging each other and keeping each other in bondage to the past. Paul demanded, "Who are you to judge someone else's servant?" (Rom. 14:4).

What a blow to their old critical way of thinking! In those days, no other person could possibly know or understand what God was doing

> Integrity is not about behavior; it is about who we are.

or demanding in another Christian's life, so they shouldn't try. They were God's servants, and He would take care of them. Their integrity was based upon their being faithful to what God was demanding of them. Something others might totally reject, yet God was demanding it! **As a Christian student, you are responsible to God and God alone for your integrity.**

A matter of integrity

We all watched as President Clinton and Starr went head to head. It was the political thunder dome: two men enter; one man leaves. We all watched him struggle when he held a press conference to apologize. He ended his apology by saying he wanted to move on. Of course he did—it was getting too hard to remember the truth. So he apologized for four minutes and then went on a vacation. As the months passed he never strayed in any of his actions. Each time he went to church he would turn to the press outside and say, "These windows were stained before I got here."

Someone once said that the greatest disappointment in the Clinton debacle was his choice of women. It's easy for us to rise up and say, "He shouldn't have done those things" or "He's lost his integrity." The truth is he probably lost his integrity before he ran for office.

In more recent days, Clinton sat with Bill Hybels in front of 4,000 people and told them that he had submitted his life to pastoral counseling and that he had begun to work at restoring his integrity. Did he mean that he had to work on not having sex? No. Integrity is not about behavior, it is about who we are. Clinton was saying that he had to come to grips with who he is in the Lord. Clinton is the son of a mother who lived a highly immoral life. He grew up seeing himself as the son of a harlot—and that is what his behavior points to. Clinton married who he wanted to be, but others outside the marriage vows were who he knew himself to be.

> Do you know who you are in the Lord? If you do, your behavior will follow, because if so, then you'll understand the significance of these words: "So then, each of us will give an account of himself to God" (Rom. 14:12).

The question is the same for each of us. Do you know who you are in the Lord? If you do, your behavior will follow, because if so, then you'll understand the significance of these words: "So then, each of us will give an account of himself to God" (Rom. 14:12).

Philosophical negativism dominates much of our culture. Little wonder we have as much compassion for trees as people, abort children for convenience, and fight to save the whales while we throw away our elderly. We have relegated man to an evolved ape, but wonder why crime dominates our streets. If life is only pleasure for a moment, why not push the envelope to the limit? If life is an accident waiting to happen, why not see how close to the edge you can go and still return?

And our response to this negativism is as pathetic as the negativism itself. The object of life is not superficial, positive thoughts or thinking better about yourself. **Saying, "I like me; I'm okay" in front of the mirror isn't going to turn your life around.** Real integrity comes from being able to accept God's opinion of you and living by that. In order to do so, you must make choices over an extended period of time in accordance with all that God has for you. You must choose to accept the significance that God has placed on your life and begin to live your life based upon that truth.

The question is, "How?" How do you come to fully believe in the worth and value that God has placed on your life? There is an answer. It can seem simple; actually it is incredibly profound.

The Believer Internalizes the Covenant Through his Behavior

In Romans 14, Paul introduces the principles that are to guide our behavior in this new covenant integrity.

THE STANDARD IS MAGNIFICENT.

"For none of us lives to himself alone and none of us dies to himself alone. If we live, we live to the Lord; and if we die, we die to the Lord. So, whether we live or die, we belong to the Lord" (Rom. 14:7-8).

We each must see ourselves as we are in Christ. This is what keeps us real in our living and authentic in our relationships. If we make the mistake of defining ourselves through success or some other external standard, then the relationships that we build will be on the basis of those external things instead of who we really are.

The danger of not understanding who we are is that no one will have a relationship with the real us. If we relate to each other on the basis of who we think the other ought to be instead of who they really are, all we are really doing is role playing. The tension in relationships comes from us not knowing who we are. The standard is we must behave on the basis of who God made us to be, not on what others think.

> When talking to someone who is not at the same place spiritually, it is helpful to ask the following three questions:
> 1. What do they know?
> 2. What do they believe?
> 3. Where are they weak?

SENSITIVITY IS THE MOTIVATION.

"Who are you to judge someone else's servant? To his own master he stands or falls. And he will stand, for the Lord is able to make him stand. One man considers one day more sacred than another; another man considers every day alike. Each one should be fully convinced in his own mind" (Rom. 14:4-5).

In the opening of the second session, I told a story about a waitress in a Mexican restaurant who gave her life to Christ. One time I was speaking somewhere, and I told that story. After I had finished, one of those highly religious, overly "spiritual" (and deeply judgmental) types came up to me and said, "Why didn't you just tell her that she was wrong to be dating that guy and that she needed to get out?" He wanted me to lay down the law to her. I said to him, "Well I don't have that right, and, besides, she just became a believer. Who am I to tell her how to live? She's doing the best she can for where she is in her life with Christ." You know, Paul is so right when he asks, disapprovingly, "Who are you to judge someone else's servant?"

We want to make everyone act a certain way and fit into a certain mold. Integrity—covenantal integrity—is not about doing what is right. It's more than that. It's a heart issue. That waitress first has to realize in her heart what God wants for her and only then will she have the strength and the desire to do it.

But too many Christians try to manipulate people's actions into what they think is right, long before their hearts have been changed. Folks, that doesn't make people love Jesus—it just makes them hate Christians. Ever thought that you might just be criticizing people because you're too lazy to pray for them?

We must learn to give people the right to let integrity be what God is developing on the inside of each person. Extend grace to others. Don't beat up on people. Let the Holy Spirit work in their lives. It's not your job to change everyone or to confront everyone's weaknesses. If there is no conviction in their lives, there will be no change no matter what you say to them. Remember that everyone you meet is in process spiritually. When talking with others, in my opinion, stay away from using phrases like, "I want to exhort you in the Lord" or "I want to confront you in brotherly love" or (my personal favorite) "The Lord told me to tell you this." These phrases are manipulative and underhanded. They represent control rather than sensitivity.

When talking to someone who is not at the same place spiritually, it is helpful to ask the following three questions:
1. What do they know?
2. What do they believe?
3. Where are they weak?

Do not let the liberty that you have received in Christ become a liability to others.

SPECIFICS MATTER.

"The man who eats everything must not look down on him who does not, and the man who does not eat everything must not condemn the man who does, for God has accepted him" (Rom. 14:3).

Because of our new covenant identity, we can expect positive, specific demands to come into our lives. The demands are there to fulfill you, not restrict you. These demands go beyond the obvious commands of Scripture. There are some things that God has said not to do: murder, adultery, abusing your body, stealing, gossiping, etc. There are demands that go beyond the "thou shalt nots." These demands come into our lives on the basis of our integrity.

Your role determines the demands that are placed on you. For example, my writing this book brings certain moral demands on me. To teach, I cannot merely give intellectual assent to certain things. The truth must come out of my life; I must live it as well as preach it.

> **The truth must come out of my life; I must live it as well as preach it.**

- As a speaker and a teacher I have to prepare—that is a specific demand—and I do so because of who I am. That's the demand of my role.
- A couple having a baby automatically become parents and take on the demands of that role.
- As a student, God has sent you to a campus, and He has certain things for you to do while you are there.
- As an athlete, the demands are set—you have to practice and you have to avoid anything that could undermine your performance in the game.
- As a member of a fraternity, which beer funnel to use is not the question—who you are and how you live in that environment is.

If you are your own person the rules are off, but if you are representing the Lord, your actions have already been determined. I have a friend who, when she started her freshman year in college, walked onto a cold unfriendly campus. She felt isolated, self-conscious, unsure, and had a desire to be accepted. Normally these four things would be the ingredients for compromise, but the Lord spoke to her and said, "If they knew who you were, they would be talking to you." He was reminding her of her identity in the Lord.

THE STRONG MUST SHOW MATURITY.

"Accept him whose faith is weak, without passing judgment on disputable matters" (Rom. 14:1).

Those of us who have walked with God the longest are responsible for the weaker ones. As the mature ones we must answer the question, "Am I willing to limit my freedom that others might come to Christ?" To choose faith over freedom and self-discipline over self-expression is maturity.

Encourage Your Group: Actions for Group Study

1. In the light of Jeremiah's stand, share what it means to be a prophet.
2. Based on the central truth of this chapter, is the CrossSeekers statement of integrity actually correct? Why or why not?
3. Take some words and make up your own politically correct translation. Try focusing on expressions that you use to hide the truth. For example, "He passed on. He's at home with the Lord." (He's dead.) Or, "We slept together. We made love." (You had sex.) Or, "I need to use the bathroom." (Don't you mean the toilet?)
4. Discuss as a group why Jesus' blood was important to the new covenant.
5. Name three promises of the new covenant.
6. What is the radical idea of new covenant integrity by your definition?
7. Compare the two statements: "He stole, so he's a thief," and "He has a heart of a thief, so he steals." Which of the two is correct? (And it can't be both.)
8. What hobby should be made an Olympic sport? Stamp collecting?

Between You and God

1. Be honest with God: Are you willing to limit your freedom so that others might come to Christ?
2. Would you rather live in the real world of TV (whatever that means) or the real world of your life? Why? Discuss this with God.
3. What is the most politically incorrect thing about your faith?
4. Prayerfully consider: Is integrity about what you do, or is it about who you are?
5. Contrast the way that you'd "exhort" and "instruct" others with how you'd want to be treated if you were caught in a similar situation.
6. Why is reducing integrity to a set of actions unhealthy?

Cold Water Crossing: The Resilient Advance In The Spirit

The Challenge
Transforming the World Through Covenant Living

Cold Water Crossing: The Resilient Advance in the Spirit

Lately I've noticed the weirdest things in stores.

I was at a convenience store, and the guy behind the counter had one of those belts you wear for heavy lifting. What's he lifting behind the counter that's so heavy—lotto tickets, cartons of cigarettes, or packages of gum?

I was in a restaurant that had a sign that said, "This is a drug free work place." Why the sign? Was there a time when they had a sign up that said, "The whole staff is toasted"? Then there's the sign in the rest room that tells employees to wash their hands before returning to work, because it is the law. The law? How about because it is good hygiene? How about saying, "After you've scrubbed the toilet, don't go make a sandwich."

I was in a stereo store that had a sign out front that read, "These doors will remain unlocked during business hours." Perhaps the owners were talking one day. One guy said to the other, "You know we haven't sold a thing since we started this business." They thought for a moment, then one guy spoke up and said, "Maybe we should unlock the doors." Right? The other one said, "For as long as we are open, let's keep them unlocked." Then the other replied, "I'll put up a sign out front so we don't forget."

There's a deli that's giving a lie detector test to its employees. I mean—sandwich artist—what is there to lie about? "Do we have any turkey?" "No, no, no. Okay, we do. I admit it, we do!"

But let's face it: people often need to hear the most obvious thing put in an authoritative manner. It's true today, and it was true in Old Testament times as well.

God was putting up big signs through ordinances and sacrifices as to how His people should live and how they should respond to Him.

The reason man was in this condition was because of what had happened in the garden.

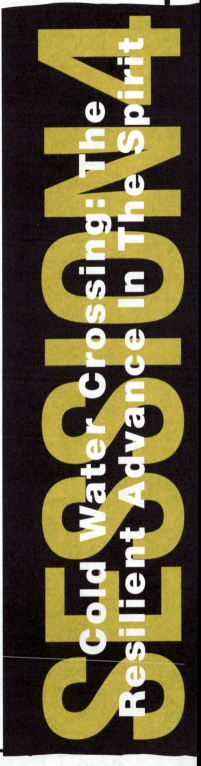

The Problem with Spiritual Growth

"In the beginning," we are given a seat in the theater of human destiny. We watch as something is formed out of nothing. We see a vision of beginning and growth as the Creator ushers in creation by bringing light, order, and life, culminating with man, the complete image of the Author of the universe.

God breathed the very life of Himself into man. In Genesis 2:7, the phrase literally means "breathed lives [plural]," meaning more than one kind of life: physical, mental, and spiritual substance. Man is given the creative opportunity to grow in every dimension of life.

Man was given boundless potential, ability, confidence, satisfaction and blessing—all found in his relationship with God. When God created the first man, He and Adam had a genuine relationship. They talked, spent time together, and even planned the future of the earth together. God loved Adam, and obviously, Adam loved God. God was meticulously concerned to meet the needs of this new man, and He did. God gave Adam complete sovereignty over the newly created world. God provided Adam with the power to subdue the earth. Most of all, God gave Adam a woman to love and be his partner. The Scripture says God saw all that He had made, "and it was good." This includes you!

God took a chance on Adam and Eve. Desiring a real relationship with this man and his wife, God placed in them absolute moral freedom. Adam and Eve had the unquestioned right to make their own choices. God restricted His choice. God refused to make them slaves. Only on the basis of complete free will could Adam and Eve be truly human. If those newly created beings were to choose to love Him and accept Him as God, it would not be compulsory. God was seeking a relationship between true spiritually related souls.

But Adam and Eve were not gods. Even though they were the apexes of creation, they were not infinite. All of creation belonged to them, but not the tree in the midst of the garden. God had placed a single restriction—a tree. It must have reminded them of their limits and God's proper place as Ruler of all.

Tragically, Adam and Eve took the magnificent possibility of having a perfect relationship with God and twisted it, misused it, and finally broke it. When they did, sin entered into creation because they sinned.

> Only on the basis of complete free will could Adam and Eve be truly human.

Their sin, like all sin, was not nebulous. It was a decisive attack against the person of God. Adam and Eve repudiated God. They personally believed a Satanic lie against God's character, and decisively rejected their relationship with Him. Satan convinced them they could be God…and they bought it. As a result of their repudiation and rejection of God, you and I have a problem. Now, at the heart of human nature, and therefore, in your heart and my heart, something is radically wrong. Since the sin of Adam and Eve, every human is born with a spirit that is alienated from God. It is controlled by sin.

Our first parents were enticed by the idea of not depending on God and living for themselves. But having bitten into the empty promises of Satan and rejecting God's promises for a full life, they fell.

What follows was the end of growth for the human race.

There was placed in the heart of mankind a consuming drive of self-reliance, self-dependence, and a deeply resentful unwillingness to submit to the call of God.

The fall brought an end to spiritual life, and indifference to God began.

The evidence that man grows physically but not morally or spiritually is seen throughout the Old Testament. In Deuteronomy 29:4, as Moses looks back on his forty years' walk with the Israelites, he writes, "To this day the Lord has not given you a mind that understands or eyes that see or ears that hear."

The seemingly insignificant decision to disobey had caused man to forfeit his ability to know God. Judging His people in Hosea 4:6, God says, "My people are destroyed from lack of knowledge." That was Israel's great undoing. Isaiah recognized man's inability to grow in Isaiah 6:9, "Who listens but does not perceive, who keeps on loving but doesn't understand." Job acknowledges man's condition in Job 33:14, "God speaks once or twice, yet no one notices it" (NASB).

If there is a "short list" of the Old Testament's influential people, Abraham, Moses, Noah, and David are there. But, as Hebrews 11:13 notes, "All these people were still living by faith when they died. They did not receive the things promised; they only saw them and welcomed them from a distance." When it came to man relating to and

> **As a result of their repudiation and rejection of God, you and I have a problem. Now, at the heart of human nature, and therefore, in your heart and my heart, something is radically wrong.**

growing in godliness, man's stubborn and inflexible heart could not achieve such a task.

In the aftermath of man's rebellion, God continued to be exceedingly patient by relating to man through sanctions, ordinances, and covenants. Like the obvious signs in restaurants and retail stores, they kept man on track until the time of the New Covenant.

THE STORY OF JOSHUA

It is easy to reduce spending time with God to a little quiet time or a time of self-indulgent, poetic journalizing and reading happy stories of other people's experiences.

As a little church guy growing up in Sunday school, I was taught that having a quiet time would get me a little gold star by my name. It became easy to be enamored by the task rather than the point of it.

In Joshua 3, God lays out the covenant plan for growing in what He asked Joshua to do with the ark of the covenant. One of the reoccurring themes of CrossSeekers is "Be More." This is the heart of God for our growth and the point of covenant living. But if we want to grow, what should be happening in our time with God? What should be the end result of time spent being with Him?

When you look throughout the Word of God, you'll find there is no place where God ever asks us to be less. The will of God is never for us to back up. The will of God is never lateral. It is always about being more. In our time with God we must hear Him calling us up to a higher place, calling us to grow for greater purpose. You will never find that God will ever say, "Okay, you're great, you're talented, you've got a lot going, but you can't do any of that."

What God does with Joshua is what God does with us in the growth of our lives day in and day out, so that we might be more. In the pursuit of our spiritual growth, there must be a resolve in our heart that says, "God I don't know what Your will is. I don't know how all the bad stuff in my life right now is going to work out. I don't know how the success and the cool stuff is going to be factored in, but—no matter what—I am committed to you to grow during the best and the worst times of my life." When we make that type of decision, God moves into our lives and works in three specific ways. **There are three things that should be happening as a result of our spending time with God: 1) He**

> In Joshua 3, God lays out the covenant plan for growing.

> God never asks us to be less.

> The will of God is always about being more.

expands His purpose for our lives, 2) He enhances our perspective, and 3) He establishes our perseverance.

In Joshua 3, Israel has been wandering around the wilderness for forty years. (Because all their leaders were men who would not stop and ask directions. Ladies, can I get an "Amen"?) Now they have finally made it to the promised land. God speaks to them saying, "Now before you take this land, I want you to take the ark of the covenant, twelve men—one from each tribe—and go stand in the waters, and I will push the waters back so that all the nations can walk across into the promised land on dry ground." They are moving out of the wilderness into the promised land. They are gaining better ground.

It's in this story that we see God's plan of growth for us.

The Plan of Spiritual Growth
1) Expands His purpose for our lives.
Joshua 3:2-4 says, "After three days as the officers went throughout the camp, giving orders to the people: 'When you see the ark of the covenant of the Lord your God, and the priests who are Levites, carrying it, you are to move out from your positions and follow it. Then you will know which way to go, since you have never been this way before. But keep a distance of about a thousand yards between you and the ark; do not go near it.'"

He is taking them in a new direction. Growth is always about moving forward. The struggle in our spiritual growth as college students is to stay out of ruts, like just reading to get information, just praying out of duty, or assuming that we have the basics down and don't need anything else. We get stuck in holding patterns that stop us from hearing and stop us from seeing and sensing the purpose of God for our lives.

I have a friend who is an interior designer. He refinishes homes. When he does, he guts out a house, redesigns the whole thing, and decorates it. I went to a house with him this week and the place was stunning. So I said, "Man, who wouldn't want to live here?" He said, "Well, I wouldn't want to live here." When I asked why, he replied, "Because I know what else I can achieve. I have something in me that is greater than this building." And I thought, "How true." We settle for so little. We think "This is great. Who wouldn't want to live here?" And God says, "If you could ever see what I had for you, you would pay any price to get it, and you would break any pattern in your collegiate/young adult life to have it." But it's so easy just to look at the circumstances and say, "I'll settle here; this will be fine." And we never dream the dreams of God. We never see all that He has for us.

So as you follow God, the way He's going to treat you is that He is going to increase your purpose. The further you walk with Him, the more responsibility you are going to have, the greater the demands are going to be, and the greater the purpose. You are moving out of the wilderness into the promised land. It's so easy to get caught up in our dreams, and we don't realize that through all the events in our lives there is the purpose of God.

See, as college students we think life is about finding a niche. "I'll get the right job and have the right person to marry and love. I'll have the right house. I'll have the right amount of money so I can afford all the things I want." We think that happiness is finding this plateau where we can retreat, and the same thing just happens day in and day out. We think we can settle into an anemic suburban happiness, but that's lateral living. It's not the purpose of God.

God is taking you to where you have not been before. It is a new place and a fresh place.

The purpose of God is that you would get to that area and that He would begin to enlarge His purposes in you and grow you up in that area.

2) He Enhances our Perspective

"The officers went throughout the camp, giving orders to the people: 'When you see the ark of the covenant of the Lord your God with the priests, who are Levites, carrying it, you are to move from your positions and follow it" (Josh. 3:3).

We all hit those times in our lives when we are panicky about knowing the will of God. We feel the pressure to know all of His will for our lives at that moment. That's not how it works. Our Christian perspective is shaped through a process.

- **It starts broad.**

Israel had walked with God for forty years by following a cloud and fire.

These things would be hard to miss, don't you think? Their relationship with God was based on the obvious. They knew God was there and they had manna every day, and they weren't dead. **This is what is commonly known as big print Christianity: See God save; see God love; see us trust Him.**

This is where we all start when it comes to growth. For us, following the cloud and the fire means bringing our lives into line morally, establishing convictions and pursuing the character of Jesus Christ. Some of us are still caught in this phase of growth, playing little beginner games and flirting with the will of God. But there will be a day when the cloud and the fire will disappear. It is God's way of challenging you to grow up.

In verse 3, he says to them, "When you see the ark of the covenant…" There are a million plus Israelites and the ark was not much bigger than a tabletop, about four feet long and two feet wide. If you were in a crowd of a million people, how easy do you think it would be to see that? I think I want a front row seat.

Yet in asking them to follow the ark, He was asking them to follow His presence. The challenge for us is that following the covenant requires more attention and more time. Now the fire, hanging high in the sky, would be hard to miss. The cloud, big in size but translucent, would take a little more effort, but it's still easy. But the ark, small in size, could only be seen with effort. Our ability to listen and obey must be refined. In this stage, it is important that we know the provisions and the blessings in each of the covenants that belong to us. Knowing what God has promised you deepens your faith and produces confidence to move forward. (Look up each of the covenants and make a list of all the promises and benefits.)

- **It moves into the specific.**

In this phase of growth, God is dealing with us in terms of desires and dreams for the future. He is building in us a vision of where our lives are headed. We must read and pray with discernment. This requires a deeper understanding and a greater focus in following the Spirit.

- **It narrows into details.**

In the last part of verse 3, God says, "You are to move out from your positions and follow it." He is giving them directions of exactly what to do. This phase of growth is the decision stage in which you begin to act on the dreams that God has crafted for you.

As we act decisively on what we know to be the will of God, other doors of opportunity—which we did not know of—begin to open. It is vital that we pass through each stage of growth in order to live covenantally.

The pattern by which God sharpens our perspectives looks like this:

It Starts Out Broad

Moves Into Specifics

Narrows to Details

It starts broad; it brings our lives under His rule.
It moves into specifics; we dream God's dreams.
It narrows into details; we are given directions.

As we look at this illustration, think of the major areas of your collegiate life and what stage you are in for each of those areas.

3) Establishes our Perseverance

In Joshua 3:7-8, God speaks and says, "Today I will begin to exalt you in the eyes of all Israel, so they may know that I am with you as I was with Moses. Tell the priests who carry the ark of the covenant: 'When you reach the edge of Jordan's waters, go and stand in the river.'" Verse 13 continues: "its waters flowing downstream will be cut off and stand up in a heap."

Joshua yelled out the command, **"We are going to stand in the water!"** So Israel entered into a giant game of pass it on, each yelling

> As long as we limit our understanding that the will of God is doing only what is possible, we will never see the full measure of the will of God.

back to the next, "We are going to stand in the water!" until it spread to all of them. Finally the message got to the guy in the very back and he said, **"What water?"**

God is moving them out of the realm of possibility into the realm of the impossible. As long as we limit our understanding that the will of God is doing only what is possible, we will never see the full measure of the will of God. As we grow up in the Lord, God is going to teach us to persevere, to stand where we are, and to obey Him fully in that situation. Perseverance is important because the will of God requires effort. It is not always immediate. It is not always automatic. There is a level of maturity required to pull it off.

What happens next in verses 15 to 16 is a very important lesson for us: "Now the Jordan is at flood stage all during harvest. Yet as soon as the priests who carried the ark reached the Jordan and their feet touched the water's edge, the water from upstream stopped flowing. It piled up in a heap a great distance away, at a town called Adam in the vicinity of Zarethan, while the water flowing down to the Sea of the Arabah (the Salt Sea) was completely cut off. So the people crossed over opposite Jericho."

So there they stood in cold, murky, overflowing water, whining to each other, "It's cold; how long do we have to stay here?" Thirty-one miles upstream, at a city called Adam, the water rose up in a heap. The minute they stepped into the water, the will of God was accomplished even though they could not see the exact means by which God accomplished His will. They stood there for twenty-four hours before all the water had flowed past them. They stood there for a day, persevering.

This is not our natural inclination. In a culture where you can buy rice that can be made in thirty seconds, persevering does not come naturally.

What most of us do is pray a prayer, give God a try, surrender to His leading, wait a nanosecond, nothing happens, so we quit. We think that if God cannot do what He needs to do within the amount of time we give Him, then we will just move on.

But part of our spiritual growth is that God teaches us that we have to stand even when we cannot see anything happening. He says to us,

> What most of us do is pray a prayer, give God a try, surrender to His leading, wait a nanosecond, nothing happens, so we quit. We think that if God cannot do what He needs to do within the amount of time we give Him, then we will just move on.

"You must stand; you must stay faithful, even if you cannot see the payoff."

This Is Life in the Major League

Our progress spiritually requires learning not to judge what God is up to based on what the circumstances look like.

Knowing how to persevere in spite of how it looks, feels, and what other people say—this is what it takes to make the cut.

The Power of Spiritual Growth

The overwhelming power of the new covenant is that it enables us to know God personally. "I will put my law in their minds and write it on their hearts" (Jer. 31:33). This is the promise that the Holy Spirit would come to live within us.

Jesus bought this privilege with His death. He gave us eternal life. With this life comes the ability to know God and grow in godliness. Jesus makes this crystal clear in His prayer for His disciples: "Now this is eternal life: that they may know you, the only true God and Jesus Christ, whom you have sent" (John 17:3).

This privilege is not to be belittled or taken lightly. It is through the work of the Holy Spirit living in us that we touch the nature of God. Paul says in 1 Corinthians 2:12, "We have not received the spirit of the world but the Spirit who is from God, that we may understand what God has freely given us."

Men lived with a fog between them and God. Their spirit was dead, so when God would speak, He sounded like one of the adults in a Charlie Brown film. God would speak, and all they heard was "wan, wan, wan, wan." It was like doing a card trick for a dog. God would say, "Here are My commands," and everyone would cock his head sideways with a puzzled look.

Jesus' death took that away. He opened up a way for our spirits to come alive for the first time since the fall. Man now had available to him the opportunity to know God for himself.

The Places of Spiritual Growth

Through this process, sensitivity is developed to God's desires and initiatives. Throughout the experiences of our lives, God's work of grace in us allows us to follow Him more closely. We must have the humility to recognize that God is continuing the process of Christianizing our own lives.

If you've been in a pillow fight recently, you know the feeling of being pummeled by a thick mushy object, leaving you with what can only be described as a dull buzz. That's exactly what happens in the spiritual journey; we've been beaten over the head when we spend time with Him. Ironically, for many, we become focused on the tasks of reading, writing in our journals, and praying for others, but in the midst of the toil, we lose sight of God, drift away from His presence, and are blind to His desires—and ourselves. Why ourselves? Well, if we lose sight of who God is, then we don't understand who we are in Him.

"You can be anything you want to be." That's what we're taught. It's the mantra that generations of American dreamers have grown up with. Self-motivated, self-reliant, self-confident—these are labels we are taught to admire. But we have forgotten what such an attitude does to the soul.

Our souls have been suffocated. There is no longer a sense of our own depravity, the severity of our need to pursue Jesus, or the importance of cultivating a life that can see Him.

Reviving the heart is the first task of spiritual growth—we must recapture the desiring heart of Psalm 42:1, "As the deer pants for streams of water, so my soul pants for you, O God." Without a heart beating from His life in us, amassing knowledge does us little good. Maturing our love for God comes in four stages: first, ignoring God; second, enjoying the provision of God; third, basking in the goodness and beauty of God; and finally, powered by His love in us, our passion is the love of God.

Second, it takes courage to get up and grow up. We bring wounds into this process. We bring our weaknesses, our temperaments, and the choices we have made. They frustrate us, but more importantly, they are obstacles in the soul's growth.

Now God is not surprised by the obstacles, and neither should we be. And we can take comfort that the One we are longing for knows us well. So feeling frustrated is not a good reason to drop out of the process. We must look at our obstacles spiritually, as God sees

> *If we lose sight of who God is, then we don't understand who we are in Him.*

> *The distractions to spiritual growth—dryness, prayerlessness, temptations, and discouragement—can do a number on us like Keith Jarett slamming us in the back of the head with a silver guitar.*

them—temporary and ready to be overcome.

 The distractions to spiritual growth—dryness, prayerlessness, temptations, and discouragement—can do a number on us like Keith Jarett slamming us in the back of the head with a silver guitar.

We must realize that God is pulling for us, yelling, "Come on! Let's keep going!" Walking, strolling, stumbling along—the call is to just keep moving forward.

The One you're walking with and the path that you're taking are secure. Your faith will grow and will ultimately result in a life that spills out into covenant living.

There is a positive motivation in spiritual growth. Even in what seems to be a negative situation, the Spirit of God always ensures progress. "Does it happen all at once?" someone asked me, speaking of spiritual growth. "No. It doesn't," I said. The Christian life is a process of cooperating with Jesus as we go along. We catch His way of doing life. In this journey we are focused followers; we are changed by His friendship.

Let's examine some of the elements which lead to distractions to spiritual growth:

DRYNESS

Often dryness comes from neglecting sin unconfessed, leaving conflicts with others unsettled, and simmering with unadmitted anger. Dryness in many ways is a breakdown in honesty between us and God. Having chosen to let things remain as they are and having chosen to keep things unspoken, it's a surprise that we'd then ask, "God why are You so silent?"

God invites us to transparency. He gives us permission to be wide open, and He clears out all that is arrogant and blasphemous in us. Opening our soul to God detoxes all the poison of sin.

Dropping our guard frees us from being shallow with God and with others. It teaches us to open up and give back to others. And it reminds us that we are His because He takes the initiative with us, not because we are clever enough to go out and find Him ourselves.

PRAYERLESSNESS

Our calendars are filled with activity, and each brings unsuspected demands that are more urgent than the ones that are actually on our calendars!

Between the emergencies and unsuspected demands, there are even more distractions, so that the quality of our prayer life is given about as much consideration as Susan Lucci at the soap awards.

At the bottom of our to do list is time for prayer, which is shameful. We assume that it doesn't require preparation, but we're wrong. We must eliminate the clutter in our lives and in our homes, so we can have both a time and a place to be with God.

We must bring our hearts to full attention, freed from distractions in our lives that keep us from having fresh faces and expectant eyes when we spend time with God. For some students this means to sit and be still; for other classmates it means to go on a walk or a run as they speak to God. Some may require silence, others a little music to drown out any background noise. Think of that guy or girl you want to spend time with. Where would you want to be if you had to have a heart-to-heart conversation about private and intimate issues? Why don't you try going there (without the guy or girl—only God)?

> Where would you want to be if you had to have a heart-to-heart conversation about private and intimate issues? Why don't you try going there (without the guy or girl—only God)?

RESISTING TEMPTATION

Everyone struggles with temptation. It's not a sign of immaturity. It's not a sin. It doesn't mean that you're a failure if you struggle with it, and it doesn't mean you've finally succeeded if you resisted—you'll face the temptation again.

It is a good way of pointing out blind spots in our lives and building a tenacious spirit to move in the opposite direction, towards God.

Seeing temptation for what it is—an opportunity for us to move away from intimacy with God, postpone our spiritual growth, and abandon for a moment the witness that we have for Christ—will help us to resist it. We want to say, "Well, I love God, but I also want to do this." Understanding temptation helps us see that we should say, "Really, if I keep doing this, knowing that it's wrong, then I'm demonstrating that I love this more than I love God."

> Seeing temptation for what it is—an opportunity for us to move away from intimacy with God, postpone our spiritual growth, and abandon for a moment the witness that we have for Christ—will help us to resist it.

And knowing this helps us to understand the best way to resist temptation—having a heart aflame to God.

DISCOURAGEMENT

We've heard the story of Noah and the flood so many times that we're

> If you are discouraged, ask yourself the following question, "What am I discouraged about?" If you ask that, I think you'll discover where your priorities are. Are you discouraged because people are saying bad things about you or because you don't have the grades or the clothes you want? If that's the case, then you don't need encouragement—you need better priorities. You need faith that God is working His good purposes in your life; and you need the patience that comes from that faith.

not touched by it, but that story shows us how to combat discouragement—with faith. Can you imagine Noah's wife? Noah went out and preached to so many people, but they would not listen; they would not repent. And his poor wife was there every day saying, "Don't worry—some people will believe you tomorrow. I'm sure that tomorrow's the day." Talk about discouragement.

But Noah was a man of faith. He knew that God would be faithful to the promise that He made. And Peter, writing in his second letter, uses Noah as an example of faithfulness—not only of man's faith in God but more importantly God's faithfulness to what He promised. God made a covenant with Noah—the first recorded covenant in the Bible—that He would not destroy the world by a flood again. But Peter writes that one day the world will be destroyed by fire, and just as no one listened to Noah, so few listen to the good news of salvation offered to us by Jesus Christ. But that doesn't mean that your faith is a failure. It just means that all you're hoping for is delayed. So, like Noah, have patience—and have faith!

Encourage Your Group: Actions for Group Study

1. Think about what you think should be the end result of reading the Bible, praying, and worshipping at church. Be prepared to share with your group.
2. Do you find that you spend time praying for the activities of spiritual growth, or do you find that you are stretched by a longing to be with Him?
3. Have each member of the group say which of the four distractions is most prevalent in his or her life—dryness, prayerlessness, temptation, or discouragement.
4. If you had to use a season in nature (fall, winter, spring, summer) to characterize your spiritual life at this moment, which one would it be? Why?
5. In our study of Joshua, we saw that God takes people where they haven't been, using whatever means necessary. Jot down one new place God is taking you right now during your college experience, and how He is getting you there. _____
_____
_____
_____

6. Is your Christian life lived like a 40-yard dash or a marathon?

Between You and God

1. Who has control over your spiritual growth?
2. In what area of your life is God asking you to be patient?
3. In what area of your life are you talking about being patient, but really you're just being lazy?
4. Think of an area in your life where you need direction, and identify where you are in the process: broad, specific, or details.
5. What's comforting about your relationship with God?

Transforming The World: It Takes More Than a T-Shirt

The Challenge
Transforming the World Through Covenant Living

Transforming the World: It Takes More than a T-Shirt

Christianity has become a subculture of trinkets and gifts bearing Christian slogans: pencils that read "My name is written in the book of life"; erasers that say "He rubs out mistakes"; tops that say, "Jesus turned my life around." The list is endless: bookmarks, cards, toys, potpourri, paintings of little cottages that, when hung in a darkened room, have a light from the cottage that seems to glow—now that may seem very devotional, but it is not new; in the 60s, pictures that glowed in the dark were called black light posters. We even have Christian candy, where each piece is wrapped in a Scripture verse. Christian candy! As opposed to that evil secular candy. Then there is Christian clothing: neckties, sunglasses that say, "I worship the Son"; Umbro soccer shorts with the logo "My Bro," along with every other commercial logo that we've stolen from Madison Avenue, stripped of any style, and stuffed full of spiritual jargon. Just whom are we trying to imitate? We live in a culture which has managed to take the mystery of God, the wonder of Jesus, and the miracle of His resurrection and reduce it to its shallowest form. We have taken the world and we have "Christianized" it.

Don't let it be said that we have Christianized or transformed everything in life except our lives and the world in which we live.

Truthfully, people don't come to Christ because they read our shirts. They come to Christ because they read our lives. Having His message written in our lives is more important than having it written on inanimate objects. What convinces people of our message is what they see of it in our lives. It's not our door mats. (I'm not kidding—I once saw a doormat that read, "All who stand here will some day stand before Him up there." I didn't see anyone kneel on that mat to accept Christ.)

Christianizing the world is not something you do; it is something you are!

Our roles as witnesses is more crucial today than ever!
We live in a world that has created a culture clash. Two worldviews are in a head-to-head, hard core battle competing for the heavyweight championship belt of the world.

The clash is pluralism vs. Christianity. Pluralism has many voices with many gods saying that all gods are equal. Its gods speak of convenience, power, expediency, and majority opinion, and they try their best to get our

attention and win our acceptance and loyalty.

"And in this corner…"

There is the Pluralist with a humanist culture insisting man makes the rules! It believes man creates good and that politics is the ultimate power vehicle for societal change. In the humanist culture everything—ethics, rules, integrity, character—is up for grabs. There is no right or wrong. Humanist culture brings about its will by either forced cooperation or simply buying people off. It has great faith that the state can solve any problem by electing people who say they will do certain things. Humanist culture looks to the government to make everything work and to make our lives better.

"And in the other corner…"

…is the Christian worldview affirming that God is in absolute control of man and his world, and that nothing will work correctly without Him. The Christian worldview deals with absolutes, rights and wrongs. It affirms that man should live by the laws of God. It insists that the world, society, and individual lives can only be changed for the better by establishing the will of God as the ruling force of each.

These two are in constant competition with each other. Deciding which worldview will win out is the heart of the struggle. It is in this battle that Christians find themselves. It is into this culture clash that we must not just bring a tract, or a little witnessing tool. In fact, we cannot just bring a message. We must live the message.

God understood this culture clash and prepared His people to win the battle. He first revealed His strategy to Abraham. In the covenant God made with Abraham He identified our role as witnesses to the world.

Covenant with Abraham

A covenant biography

God came to Abraham while he lived in Haran, and He promised to protect him, provide for him, and prosper him. Look at the following points in this man's life.

- Aged, Abraham wondered if he could ever have a son.
- God's voice broke the silence: "Abraham, count the stars." I can

> Christianizing the world is not something you do; it is something you are!

> These two are in constant competition with each other. Deciding which worldview will win out is the heart of the struggle.

almost hear Abraham replying, "Lord, you count them. You are already up there. Besides I cannot count that high."
- God spoke again, "As many stars as there are, that's how many your descendants shall be."
- God continued, "I brought you to this land, and I will make a covenant. I will make you exceedingly fruitful. I will make nations of you, and kings will come forth from you."
- Abraham and Sarah were both anxious for the day when God would come and fulfill His promise to them. She was 75, and he was 85.
- Abraham traveled south to Negev and found new pasture. This was many years after the birth of Ishmael. It was here that Sarah gave birth to God's promised son, Isaac (Gen. 21:1-3).
- Then God said, "Take your son, that I know to be the love of your life, and offer him on Mt. Moriah." Abraham, now well into his nineties, had learned to trust God (Gen. 22:2-3).
- Early the next morning on Mt. Moriah Abraham laid Isaac on the alter and raised his knife to kill the boy with a single stroke (Gen. 22:9-10).
- "Abraham," God called to him. "Yes Lord," he answered, as he held the knife over his head. "Don't hurt the boy." Abraham looked just beyond the altar and saw that God had provided a ram for the sacrifice.
- Again the Lord spoke, "I will bless you and multiply your descendants as the stars. By all the nations of the earth you will be blessed." Since that moment, **God has provoked the world to jealousy with the blessings that He bestows on the lives of His people** (Gen. 22:11-13,15-18).

First Corinthians 4:20 says, "The kingdom of God is not a matter of talk but of power." The power of God rests on the lives of the believers—not in some freaky weird way but in the fullness of God in the form of His blessings—that the world might see His blessings in our lives, that others are drawn to discover God's life for themselves.

Just how are people provoked by the blessings of God that are on our lives? They are provoked by the following four things, and it's important that we understand the basis and benefits of each. Let's examine these four things.

1. RESOLVED TO THE RULE OF CHRIST
The Basis: Examine Ephesians 4:5-10.

What God did through David was to establish Christ on His throne as Ruler overall. In the New Testament, the apostle Paul picks up on this in

Ephesians 4:5, when he speaks of "one Lord, one faith." In verse 6, he continues his thought when he says that there is "one God and Father of all, who is over all and through all and in all." A covenant commitment involves the recognition that Jesus is the Son of God and the Savior of humankind.

As God's witnesses, we are not here to establish the rule of Christ. It has already been established. That's what Paul is saying in the above verses. Christ already reigns. Regardless of who is in office, or what laws are passed, Jesus rules. He rules over everything.

As a Christian student, realize this is one thing that we do not get to vote on. No matter what stand society takes on moral issues, Jesus still rules.

The Benefits

When we follow the rule of Christ, good things happen. The blessing of God comes on our lives. As we live in the blessing of God, people see it and ask, "How does this happen in your life?"—to which we reply, "It's the blessing of God." When people see the rule of Christ in our lives and its blessings, they are drawn to it. And so, we Christianize and transform the world. You now have the basis and the benefits. If you are a Christian, seek to live a life which follows the rule of Christ so closely that other students see the blessing of God in you.

2. REGULATED BY THE RULE OF CHRIST
The Basis: Examine Ephesians 4:13.

Paul not only addresses the rule of Christ over all and in all believers in Ephesians 4, but he also addresses the role of the citizens of the kingdom. In Ephesians 4:13, Paul writes that we are to "reach unity in the faith and in the knowledge of the Son of God and become mature, attaining to the whole measure of the fullness of Christ."

Everybody is regulated by something: emotions, desires, childhood, or habits. Covenantal believers are regulated by the beautiful, wonderful, and triumphant rule of the King.

Through His power and presence we learn to control ourselves. As witnesses we don't believe in attitudes like, "Hey, I can do whatever I want" or "If I want it, I can have it." Self-control means that we don't give ourselves free rein; we are disciples—disciplined ones.

To say, "I am waiting for God to change me," "I can't help it," or "It's just the way I grew up" misses the point. **They're just lame excuses.**

Understanding that God has placed in you a spirit of self-control eliminates that type of thinking. **Resident within you is the power of God.** Your life does not have to be out of control. This is the essence of covenant living. The Spirit of God brings inspiration and motivation in us for self-control.

To be good witnesses we must learn to govern our lives. "That may be all well and good," you may be asking, "but how do I get self-control?" Your witness will be consistent with your actions.

The Benefits

The blessing of God in self-control is the ability to trust our hearts and have confidence in our own desires. The psalmist hits it right on the head when he says, "Delight yourself in the Lord and He will give you the desires of your heart" (Ps. 37:4). In other words, fully give God your heart, and then you can trust your heart, and your desires will be His desires.

An uncontrolled person cannot witness effectively by trusting his emotions, thoughts, or desires. He looks at the disciplined ones and sees their lives marked by decisive authority and a lack of fear and timidity because Christ rules their lives. Their witness is consistent with God's desire for their lives. When the uncontrolled person observes this type of controlled living, a desire to know the God of self-control is created.

3. REPRESENTATIVES OF THE RULE OF GOD IN OUR WORLD

We are to represent man before God and God before man. As a Christian student, regardless of what you and I may think about where God has us—no matter how small the dorm room or how tedious the classes may be, we represent God. The big question is: How are we representing God where He places us? Are we speaking up in God's name in the middle of our campuses and our culture and classrooms? Are we God's representatives?

The Basis

In this world we need believers who understand that they are not separate from the will of God. In the major that you pick, whatever your hobbies may be, whatever you choose to do with your life, and whatever role you play in the world, your primary responsibility is to be a witness to others of the the presence of God.

> **Resident within you is the power of God. Your life does not have to be out of control. This is the essence of covenant living.**

> **Whatever you choose to do with your life, and whatever role you play in the world, your primary responsibility is to be a witness to others of the the presence of God.**

As representatives of the King and His Kingdom, our lives must be characterized by excellence in everything we do. If there is one thing we know about God, it is that He is the Creator. He loves work that is well done and loves to see it in the lives of His people. Just as nature speaks of the beauty of God, so do our lives.

God desires that we be the most creative we can be, whatever our function in life. This includes areas like the arts, music, and business. Can you see how God wants you to bring Him honor and be His witness through your chosen field of study?

The Benefits

Transforming and Christianizing the World

To function properly as God's representative means that His blessings will flow through you. Being God's representative wherever He places you insures that the blessings of God will be in your life and flow out of your life. This provokes others to inquire about Christ for themselves. Representing God in society has enormous implications in every level of life: our personal lives, our families, the church, our campuses, and the culture in general.

As God's representatives, students impact other people as well as ministers do. As God's representatives, we live the standard of a God-centered life. A friend's brother is a doctor, but he's currently pursuing a degree in philosophy and theology at a prestigious divinity school. Why? Because he wants to speak on ethical issues to the medical community and to the world. He wants to be a voice for Christ to doctors, and he wants to speak for Christ as a doctor. Here's someone who has spent years and years in the university so that he can be a doctor, and now he's there again, seeking the understanding found in Scripture for the moral questions raised by his medical practice. He could have said, "Well, being a doctor will give me the chance to meet people and maybe then I'll get a chance to witness to them that way," but he has a vision that goes beyond that. He sees that speaking as God's representative is the purpose of his whole life—not just something he does when he's not being a doctor. He is doing this—turning away from the big bucks to become a student again—because he follows the standard of a God-centered life.

Our world is chaos. It is in a mess because we have lost that standard for living. Everyone has his own opinions, ideas, inclinations, and preferences on what he should do and how he should live. In the middle of that

> Being God's representative wherever He places you insures that the blessings of God will be in your life and flow out of your life.

kind of society, we must communicate the truth and uphold the standard so that people can know the life of God and receive the blessings of God for themselves.

4. REFLECT THE RULE OF GOD IN OUR SOCIETY

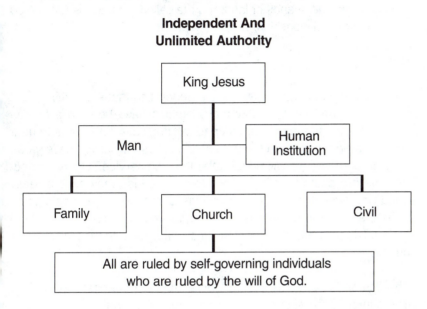

> The goal of covenant living is to bring believers to a point of maturity, in which their lives are conformed to the heart of God.

We are citizens of a theocracy who are ruled through covenant. The rule of God is established on this earth in three areas: family, church, and civil government.

The Basis

Family

Ephesians 5:22 says, "Wives, submit to your husbands, as to the Lord." Verse 25 says, "Husbands, love your wives, just as Christ loved the church and gave himself up for her." Talk about reflecting the rule of God within covenantal relationships! Anyone who has been on a mission trip to another country will tell you it is far easier to witness to a stranger than it is to his spiritual or biological family.

The ultimate goal of covenantal families is that other families would see the blessing of God on that family and want it for themselves.

As students, we want to sacrifice our lives for Christ and heroically pronounce that we will take a bullet for Christ. At the same time, we have no problem using each other in our relationships and having noncommittal make out sessions. We dream of dying intensely for the name of Christ and being martyred, but we never give a second thought to how we treat our parents and hold grudges against relatives. You are not called just to witness to people in another land. You are called to bring the will of God into all of your relationships, single or married.

Church

When it comes to church, we have a generation that kinda mixes and matches. I can't tell you how many times I have been in a church speaking, and someone comes up to me and says, "We came to hear you this morning, here at the 9:30 service." I usually say, "That's great. Stay around, and we will go eat after the next service." They respond, "No, we are going to drive across town, because they have a really good worship leader." So what happens is that there are people going to hear a speaker at one church, going to sing at another church, and then driving across town to eat lunch with their friends at another church.

The church is not to be another social club, but the alternate society. The church is the seat of the government of God in the earth.

The church's role is to transform and Christianize the world through its people. The church is made up of covenantal representatives who are righteous men and women who take their drive, zeal, and passion for Christ and His church into the world. By doing so, they provoke the world to jealousy because of the success that rests on their lives. That is the ultimate witness.

God is building a whole new community in the church. So much of what God wants to do in your life personally cannot happen in isolation. Not all the promises of God are given to you individually; some are given corporately.

But as you, the individual, are related to the city of God, then all the promises become yours.

So many lives are falling apart and are in a mess because of our relationship with God. We need to seek a relationship with the community of God.

> The ultimate goal of covenantal families is that other families would see the blessing of God on that family and want it for themselves.

> The church is not to be another social club, but the alternate society. The church is the seat of the government of God in the earth.

Part of our role as witnesses is not to see church as something that we skip in and out of, or a place that we go to until we get offended by someone's illustrations or sermons, or until we don't approve of the style of music or they don't do the right choruses from our favorite CD; then we leave. That is not what church is about. *Part of our role as witnesses is being planted in a church and finding our identity in a body. Out of this identity we are sent into society as witnesses.*

Civil

We are to establish and to reflect the rule of God, not just in family and in church but also in the **civil areas** of life, which means work and politics. To the extent that people make decisions based on the will of God determines the godliness of our society or our workplace.

God puts into place the principle of governing authorities but does not necessarily endorse everything those authorities do. We understand that even when bad people hold offices they do so with the permission of God. Could God be calling you into a career in government or politics? Are you prepared to be a witness for Christ in this way?

Whenever a society such as a university gets away from God's Word as a moral index, man will begin to mix man's laws and God's laws. Man's laws will always be subjective. Look at government and ask if God would let some laws pass that we have now. How did they pass? Can you think of a law on the books right now which does not glorify or reflect the character of God? Some who are not in a meaningful relationship with God will ask, "Why does God let something like this happen?" Remember, all humans can choose! That's the way God works.

When God establishes His rule, He does not come down to dictate to us; we still have to choose. When He says, "I set before you life and death," we still have to choose whether we follow God's will or our own.

The willingness of the governed to be submitted to the law of God determines how Christian the nation is. That is true in business, and that is true in politics.

In Summary

The principle of witnessing is that the world sees our relationship with

> **But as you, the individual, are related to the city of God, then all the promises become yours.**

Christ and the blessings it brings, and is enticed to ask about it. This is how divine appointments are created. Our witness is determined by what others have seen of Christ in our lives. This is what Peter had in mind when he wrote in 1 Peter 3:15, "Always be prepared to give an answer to everyone who asks you to give the reason for the hope that you have." What about your life provokes others to want to know Christ? What would you like to see in other Christians? Part of what we are dealing with is the foundation of covenant living...that is accountability under Christ.

5. RELATED TO EACH OTHER UNDER THE RULE OF CHRIST

It is not made up. It is not something that is going to take place way out in the distance after Tim LaHaye runs out of things to write. The rule of Christ is very real and very, very present. The question is, "How do we see that rule on this earth?" How is the invisible made visible? How is the intangible made tangible? How is it that the heavenly become seen among the earth? The covenant, the rule of Christ, and the will of God show up **through His people**.

Christ rules, but He chooses to rule through us and in us. The way we experience the rule of God in our lives is by submitting to the hierarchy that God has established. Once this happens, we don't question whether we witness or not. Our lives are witnessing daily.

In Deuteronomy 1, Moses says, "How am I to govern these people? The task is too great for me." In verses 13-15, he begins to set up the hierarchy. Why is that important to us? Because the way we touch the power of God, the way that we know the blessings of God, and the way we hear the voice of God comes through this hierarchy.

To come into covenant means that you come under authority. Our generation believes that church is optional, the body is optional, and that it's all between Jesus and me. As long as I am right with Jesus, as long as we are okay, then everything else is all right. That's just not true. This is not the witness God desires our lives to convey to a lost world.

God's Word teaches us to honor the presence of authority. God rules through people. Our actions, thoughts, and experiences all witness to the reality of God in our lives. It blows my mind when I hear all these students on daytime talk shows and they mouth off to their parents and say, "Who died and made you God?" I want to yell, "Well, God did." He placed parents over us, and He placed other authorities over us. God knew that our parents would be tough to deal with. Maybe that's why He doesn't command us to love them—but He does ask us to honor them.

We don't obey them because they are good people or because they are always right; we obey them because they represent the authority of God in our lives. Even if they are not godly, they are still our parents. God wants us to honor and respect them. When we honor them, we are worshipping God. We are not condoning their lifestyle or actions by honoring them; we are following God's guidelines for our lives. As members in the church, we are not free just to rail on the pastor and to get up in his face. We are under the pastor's authority. It staggers me when I see people walk into church—even people who are not members of that church—and they feel like they have the freedom to condemn, reprove and critique someone in ministry, when in reality those leaders represent the authority of God.

> **We need to remember that the rule of God can be seen in all of our relationships and demonstrate our witness.**

We are all under someone else's authority. If it's not our parents, it's teachers. If it's not pastors, it's a boss. God puts people in our lives over us to represent His authority and to teach us how to honor authority because, as we honor authority, we honor the God who placed them over us. Instead of swaggering up to your local minister and yelling, "I don't approve" or "You're a jerk!" we must honor the people that God has placed in authority over us. We need to remember that the rule of God can be seen in all of our relationships and demonstrate our witness.

So whether we honor someone or not is not subjective. We don't do it because they deserve it or because they please us or because they are right. It is even as we honor people that are jerks, or stupid, that our response to the rule of Christ is seen. Can you see the importance of your lifestyle being a part of your witness for Christ?

So this hierarchy teaches us to honor the presence of God. Not only that, but **it also holds us personally accountable**. Verse 13 of Deuteronomy 1 says, "Choose some wise, understanding and respected men from each of your tribes and I will set them over you." This is not a Jesus and me thing.

> **Your personal success depends upon your relationship to the church.**

Someone else's bad decision doesn't give us the right to be bad in return. What's at stake when we say this? Look at yourself in the mirror. What do you see? It's a reflection of who you are physically. Your witness reflects who you are spiritually. Transforming the world takes more than a T-shirt!

> **Part of what we are dealing with is the foundation of covenant living...that is accountability under Christ.**

> So our witness is that in a relationship
> - when we have been abandoned, we reconcile;
> - when we are abused, we pray for them;
> - when they are unfaithful, we forgive;
> - when they break the law, we confront;
> - when they bless us, we thank them.

Just because someone else does wrong, doesn't give us the right to contribute to the breakdown of relationships and to contribute to the darkness of the world.

Biblical principles are to order our lives and to help focus our witness for Christ. They hold us personally accountable for our actions and our responses towards everyone…even the students whose lifestyles we hate.

Finally, our witness results in a holy and practical accomplishment. Verse 8 says, "See, I have given you this land. Go in and take possession of" it. What does witnessing for Christ bring into our lives? It forms maturity. We become people with order and focus in our lives. When we learn how to submit to the leading of God as He reaches out to a lost world, society benefits. The world is able to see Jesus. How do the blessings of God show up on your campus?

Our generation must stop thinking like daytime talk show people who have the right to battle it out with everyone around us who we don't agree with and take up some offense about how certain people act.

Covenant people will honor the desires of Christ. We will be held personally accountable in how we respond to a world without Christ. We need to have faith that honoring the will of Christ to love all people will result in a holy and practical accomplishment.

Encourage Your Group: Actions for Group Study

1. Are you thinking strategically about your life? How will what you are doing now help you be on mission with God and witness through your choices? Share with those in the group if appropriate.
2. On a scale of one to ten, would you say that your life is characterized by excellence in sharing the good news of Christ's love with others? (1 = No Excellence; 10 = Complete Excellence.)

3. Can Christian paraphernalia get in the way of us being witnesses? Do you really think that someone wearing a t-shirt saying, "Buddha—that's my final answer" would make you consider being a Buddhist?

Between You and God

1. Which of the four areas—determining your life beliefs, resolving your personal problems, settling unfinished emotional hurts, and staying out of fantasy—holds you back from being a full and effective witness for Christ? What can you do about it? Better yet, what can God do about it?
2. Make a note of three characteristics that describe the person who led you to Christ. See how many of those deal with what he or she said and how many deal with who that person is.
3. Pray that God will help you see that being the message is just as important as having the message.
4. Discuss your motive for witnessing with God. (And if you see it as a duty, then no wonder why you never do it.)

Brick by Brick: Building The House of God

Brick by Brick: Building the House of God

When we think of church, it's usually in terms of experiences. I occasionally have flashbacks of pot luck dinners—how can we as Christians be against gambling and for pot lucks? A pot luck is a dinner which is made up of dishes that have been cryogenically entombed in a church member's freezer for decades. They have been saving these dishes for just such an occasion. I believe the "pot" in "pot luck" is an acronym for "petrified, overcooked, and tasteless." You remember the combinations: lasagna and meat loaf; twenty-bean salad; Spam; cold green beans; and brownies that were actually divots from the men's golf tournament.

The experiences of church that make us laugh are too many to mention, but there's one that sticks out in my mind: the church bus that was always in need of repair. No matter how much work was done on it before the trip, it would break down. Some of the fondest memories I have of our youth group are relationships that we formed while standing on the side of some random highway waiting for the tow truck to come.

To this day there are still things I would like to see in the church: a shark fin floating behind the pastor while he is baptizing; deacons throwing money at the congregation during the offering; people doing the wave during the sermon (somebody else's sermon, please!); bathrooms labeled "First John" and "Second John" with a picture of Charlton Heston hung between the two doors that says, "Let my people go."

The point of this rant (and there is a point) is that when we think of church we think in terms of how we have been affected by it. This chapter is about how we affect church. *We cannot understand ministry in any aspect apart from the covenantal view of service.*

1) The Picture of Service is Painted in the Davidic Covenant

In a day in which ministry has become entrepreneurial, when there are many who are out there doing their own thing, it's vital that we see service in the kingdom as the continual fulfilling of God's covenant with David, who was promised an everlasting kingdom. Service is about more than signing up for a task. It involves your whole life. You and your service are connected to the covenant. It's crucial that we understand each element of service in view of our place in the covenant.

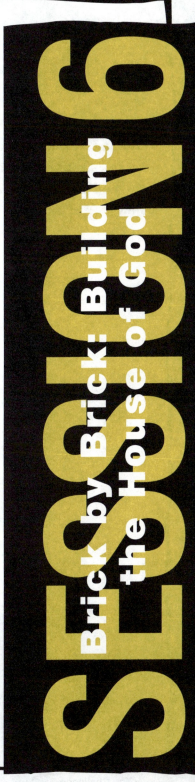

> Service is about more than signing up for a task. It involves your whole life. You and your service are connected to the covenant.

A covenant biography
Check out these facts from the life of David.
- The Israelites had come and anointed David as the next king.
- Something began to stir in David's heart, and David was restless.
- David knew Jerusalem was where he needed to reign.
- The Israelites were members of David's kingdom, and they settled there. This was the city of David's throne—the place from which God would rule.
- David's kingdom was the envy of all who saw it.
- One night, as David looked out over his kingdom from his palatial estate, he spoke to the Lord: "I have all this beauty and this wonderful house, but you dwell in a tent. I must build a place for you."
- In response, God inverted David's request and said, "No, David. I will build you a house." And what God had in mind was far greater than a palace made of stone. It was far more reaching than just what David could see. God would establish David's rule to all generations.
- Revelation 11:15 looks forward to its completion when it says, "The kingdom of the world has become the kingdom of our Lord and of Christ, and he will reign forever and ever." The son of David will rule people that come from every tongue, tribe, and nation.

God has chosen to rule the world through people. That's why David's throne in the Old Testament is called the throne of God and why God's throne in the New Testament is called the throne of David. David understood the impact of this. It thrilled him and gave him great joy; it seems natural that David was dancing before the Lord with all his might (2 Sam. 6:14). God promised David a house. And God's house has David's son, the Lord Jesus, sitting on the throne.

Jesus comes to *build* a house—not to rebuild a house—and this house is built using material no one had ever thought of.

2) Polish up on the Standards

"Hey, how do I start speaking? I've got a testimony that I believe can make a difference for God." "I need to be an evangelist because I want to make an impact in the world and not just in one church." "I am wasting my talents here in this little church." "There is nothing I love more than singing on stage, worshipping Him."

In all the places ministry has taken me, I too often hear these things said. The only thing more frightening than these statements is the number of I's that are found in them. I've seen eye charts with less I's in them.

The Challenge
Transforming the World Through Covenant Living

But I've (there's the I again!) said some of these things myself.

Just because you can get a hamburger any way you want it, doesn't mean you can order ministry on your own terms. Our culture of instant gratification has resulted in a great deal of superficial service. Jesus didn't start spouting off profound things and go on the road to show off. His life had been tested and tried. He started His ministry late, after doing an ordinary blue collar job, and after studying the Scriptures all of His life!

Our attraction "to making it" or "getting the big break in ministry" has blinded us to the fact that service works on unchangeable principles. Service apart from these principles misses the reason for the call of God on your life.

Let's look at **four standards for service.**

First, we serve through the church to the people.
One of the most startling statements I have heard from thousands of young adults who surrender to full-time ministry communicates that we think Christian service is about leadership, not about service.

The dominant word when describing service is "egalitarianism," which means that everyone is equal. To believe that means that everybody can see themselves as independents: "me serving God on my own conditions." The whole idea behind the Davidic Covenant is that the ultimate rule of the Son of David would have structure to it. *We cannot serve as independent contractors; we have to serve in the context of God's house.*

In covenantal service one cannot be anti-church and pro-God. The desire of God is to build the church, and we must be controlled by the Father's desire. Jesus was directed by the dream of God. Often He would say, "I can only do what I see my Father doing." As His disciples, we must do what the Son is doing.

Our motivation for serving is not people. It's serving God. If the focus of service is people, then we should join the Red Cross. As church people we have grown up with the understanding that service is being where the people are and understanding how we meet with them. But that's not covenant service. As people of the covenant, our service is to build the house of God.

Second, our gift won't work outside of the church.
"I've outgrown the church. It doesn't really do anything for me anymore." "The church is for my parents, but it's not really for me." These are things often spoken by your generation. Covenant is concerned with an acute focus on the will of God. Everything in our lives is determined by it. In the area of service it is vital to remember that there is a King we serve.

No one individual has all the answers or solutions. That is why there is the church. We serve as a team. To serve apart from building God's house is to leave the reason for service unfulfilled.

In Christendom today many of the heroes building the ministry are not churchmen. What they are doing is not locked into a community. They don't recognize the authority of the church and its place in the world. They are more than willing to use the church for financial gain and building attendance for their meetings, but they are not serving the church. They want to help people but not the church. What is shocking about this is that it is possible to build something that is fantastic and financially healthy but, because it's not locked into the care of the church, misses the goal of covenant service.

We need a new generation of covenantal believers who will be about serving the purpose of God in and through the church. What you love to do may bring you joy and energy and come with great ease, but it is not yours to do with whatever you want. Our gifts are not our own; they have corporate value. They exist to benefit the building plans of God. The value of your gift furthers God's plans, and it will not work as it should outside of its designated domain, the church.

Third, our gift is connected to other gifts.
Your gift is not just about you. Paul shoots up a flare for clarity in Ephesians 4:16 when he says, "From him the whole body, joined and held together by every supporting ligament, grows and builds itself up in love, as each part [that's you and me] does its work."

Service is not a solo sport.

The usefulness of your gift grows in the context of the church. To the extent that God can trust you to serve in His body will determine the enlargement of your service in the kingdom.

The further we get away from church the more dangerous our gift becomes, i.e, check your history books for Jim Jones, David Karesh and the Heavens Gate people—need I say more? I think I will. I once had a guy say to me, "You know, I am a really gifted speaker. God just gives me my messages, so I don't need to study." To which I said, "So you just shoot from the hip and hope you don't blow your foot off?" This guy is one ladle away from drinking Kool-Aid.

- Staying connected to others in the church keeps our doctrine strong and our theology sound.
- It keeps us from believing that we can get to heaven on a space ship.

Fourth, a fully functioning church equals Christ Jesus in the world. Why did Jesus say, "Greater things will you do than me" (John 14:12)? When Jesus stepped into this world, He limited Himself to time and space by taking on the restrictions of humanity. He was only able to be in one place at one time. By gifting His church with His gifts, which they carry into the entire world, the presence of Christ can now be every place on earth at one time through His church.

When every believer knows his gift and understands it—his role in the body—he will understand clearly that the goal of service is to build God's house. When that happens, the rule of God is extended throughout the world. The strategy is progressive.

Start with a person
　Populate families
　　Build churches
　　　Change neighborhoods
　　　　Influence cities
　　　　　Fill counties
　　　　　　Impact states
　　　　　　　Cover nations
　　　　　　　　Take the world

3) Why People are Scared of Serving

It often puzzles me when I hear people say, "I've always known God wanted me to be serving Him, but that was years ago and I had to get on with life." If God had spoken so clearly to them then why wouldn't they do what He said to do? Why would you draw back from service? The answer is found in one simple, yet very powerful word: fear. People are afraid of service. Let's look at the list of fears below and see what keeps you from serving.

> By gifting His church with His gifts, which they carry into the entire world, the presence of Christ can now be every place on earth at one time through His church.

> The greatest danger we face in building the kingdom is that we would serve but disqualify ourselves because of our personal life.

Disconnect
"Whatever I might do won't be enough, and it won't make a difference."

We make service something that doesn't exist in ordinary life, something only being done overseas or inside the church building. But service does include life in the marketplace—for example, when you help others on your own time. Titus 3:2 encourages acts of service that we would "show true humility toward all men." In our increasingly high-tech society the human touch is greatly needed.

If you are alive you can serve.

Dodge
"I don't know if I can do it."

Buried not far beneath this statement is the fear of failure. "What if I fail?" "What if I let God down?" This is the biggest fear there is because it paralyzes us from serving God. There is an element of risk in serving God. Your success in service is in facing that risk and saying to God, "I'll go ahead and do it," trusting that He will equip you as you obey. Don't be afraid. Whatever God asks you to do will work. **You cannot take the risk of being out of the will of God.**

Service is not always about being safe.

But fear has a fear. Fear's greatest fear is that you would obey the will of God because it knows that when you do, it will lose its power over you. Someone once said,

> *"Feel the fear and do it anyway."*

Initially you will have to step out, but once you do, confidence in what God is asking you to do will began to rise.

Discount
"There are others who can do it better."

This statement holds up about as well as a balsa wood chair in Paul Perdone's kitchen. The idea that there are "special Christians" and that the average Christian is not called to serve is just not true. If we don't serve as one in covenant, then we build our lives apart from the plan of God.

This particular fear has its roots in comparison. It exaggerates others' abilities in our eyes and makes us believe that what we have to offer is not good enough. This is not true. From God's perspective, **what's inside of you is unique and important to the kingdom.** God affirms that your life is a resource: you can serve and do it wonderfully.

Stop disqualifying yourself and believing the limitations that have been placed on your life. Believe that you can do what God is asking you to do.

Devalue
"I know it is important, but it is not my problem."

We make the same mistake with service by not internalizing it. We have intellectualized it, understood the statistics, and seen the videos, but we fail to make the connection to the heartbeat of God. When Scripture speaks of service it never leaves us with just the theological explanation. It always goes straight to the human heart in relationship to God. Your life and your resources are vital to what God is doing on the earth. It is your problem, and you are the solution.

Disassociate
"Hey, I'm doing all I can do."

One of my favorite worship choruses is "We Are Hungry." There is a line that says, "Lord I want more of You." We desire that God would give us all that He has and that our lives would be filled with His blessings, yet what do we give back to Him? Every time I sing that line, I always imagine Him leaning down and saying, "No, more of you." How much of you does God have? Would you say it was 74 percent, 85 percent, 96 percent, or 100 percent?

There is no limit to what God can demand of us. If God only owns a part of us, then we are living in denial of the fact that we have been bought at a price and that we are not our own.

4) Paradigm Shift
Imagine for a moment what it would be like to be homeless. You've left school. You have no money. You have no family. Just a random person with no real belongings, marginalized by society and for the most part overlooked. That's what it was like to be a Christian in the days of Peter. Check it out.

- The Jews regarded Christians as nobodies and shunned them because of their belief in Jesus as the Messiah.
- Peter writes to these "homeless Christians" and leads them into a new and wonderful discovery.
- Peter opens his letter in 1 Peter 1:1 by referring to these people as "scattered," which could have been secret decoder ring talk for "the Israel of God."
- Then, in chapter 2, verse 5 of his first letter, he refers to them as "living stones…being built into a spiritual house." He is telling them that they are the new temple of God.
- Peter intentionally uses four phrases from the Old Testament to teach them who they are. In verse 9 he says they are "a chosen people, a royal priesthood, a holy nation, a people belonging to God."
- These phrases are important because originally they were used to characterize natural Israel as God's people. Peter uses them to drive home the point that the living stones of Christ are God's new Israel.
- This is the paradigm shift that Peter is emphasizing: it's not about physical Israel but about the spiritual Israel who are the living stones. These living stones are the fulfillment of the promise that God gave to David.

Because of our union with Christ, who is the foundation, each of us, being living stones, must use our status in service of God's house to Christianize and transform the world. In verse 5, Peter gives the reason for our roles as living stones when he says, "to be a holy priesthood, offering spiritual sacrifices acceptable to God through Jesus Christ." We have been made to serve.

5) Placing the Stones

It was the beginning of the fall semester, and room 307A was filled to capacity. In walked a man with silver gray hair, wearing a weathered blue work shirt, British made khakis, and brown chukka boots. He threw his well-worn leather satchel on the desk, and the thud that it made was not the thud of books. All the students turned to look as the teacher unsnapped the flap of the satchel. From it, he took a brick. As he held it high over his head he said, "This is a brick," and with his other hand he pointed to a series of lithographs of cathedrals and mansions that hung behind him. "These are all made out of bricks. A brick wants to belong. The primal urge of this brick is to be used as a part of something greater than itself. Ladies and gentleman, your job is to figure out where the bricks belong. Let's get started." As living stones, the task that lies before us is to figure out where we fit, and into what part of the structure we belong. God the Architect has a plan and a design, and we must know where we fit in that design.

Every Christian student on your campus has at least one spiritual gift. Unlike the gifts your friends and family may have given you, you cannot return this one.

6) Powering up for Service

Expectancy and trepidation coexist in the call to serve. We look forward to participating in and seeing the fulfillment of what God has called us to do, yet there is the presence of our weakness and inexperience in serving proficiently.

If you have ever felt this way, then you are not alone.
- Timothy faced the same thing. He felt that he was far from ever being a saint, and he believed himself to be unqualified for the heavy task Paul was placing on him. Yet at the same time he knew God had called him, and he had always longed to serve.
- It is important to note that Timothy is not taking this service independently but rather because of his commitment to the house of God.
- Paul is helping a living stone (Timothy) find out what to do and how to do it.
- The reason these letters are in the Word of God is because what Paul is saying is meant for us.
- Everyone needs a spiritual father to encourage and motivate them to serve. Let Paul be yours, take these words personally, and let them sink into your life.
- Paul writes Timothy a positive, motivational letter urging him to confidently step into the service that God has for him. What Paul is doing through these letters is getting Timothy ready to serve.

To be effective in service you must see your whole life in relation to that call.

Recognition of the call to service
1 Timothy 1:18: "Timothy, my son, I give you this instruction in keeping with the prophecies once made about you, so that by following them you may fight the good fight."

- For Timothy, the task of pastoring a church in Ephesus, a city known for its pagan worship, was a difficult assignment. It would have been easy for him to step away from such a task. In this verse Paul is reminding him of the greatness of his destiny. He is challenging Timothy to believe what has been said about him through the prophecy of his call. With the voice of a general speaking to a soldier, Paul tells Timothy, "You can do this. Don't forget that you are a man under orders. Obedience is not an option; God has chosen you."

- There is a supernatural equipping that God places in every individual life. Confidence for service comes from knowing the call of God that rests on our lives. God's sovereign idea for our lives is greatness. We each must recognize it in our own lives and embrace it for ourselves. This call serves as the great map of our lives. **God is doing something supernatural when we serve.**
- When I first began the Metro Bible Study in Houston, my greatest fear was that no one would come back after the first night, and I felt that way every week following. My spiritual father told me something I have never forgotten—he said, "You must always remember that **you are God's man with God's message for that moment** and you must walk confidently in that truth." That advice has helped me to serve faithfully for many years. It is from the recognition of your gift that you are able to fight the good fight.

The requirement of service
1 Timothy 4:6: "…brought up in the truths of the faith and of the good teaching that you have followed." What Paul was talking about in 1 Timothy 1:18 is worked out in this verse. He is telling Timothy to do something with his call.

- The knowledge of the call gives purpose and direction, telling you what to make a priority in your life. You must commit yourself to specific actions to fulfill what you believe God is telling you to do.
- For many students, the call of God is only a desire, a dream, and an idea. Regardless of what you are doing, whether it is sacking groceries or scooping french fries, you still have to do other things in order to fulfill that call.
- Paul was well acquainted with this principle. He was a tentmaker by trade, but he did not make tents in order to corner the tent market. He did it to fulfill the apostolic call that was on his life. He had many people that traveled with him, and he had to provide for them.

In the kingdom it all counts: we are buying tomorrow by what we do today.

The role of service
1 Timothy 4:14: "Do not neglect your gift, which was given you through a prophetic message…"

- Paul reminds Timothy of his spiritual gift and God's special place of his service and ministry. Timothy had been ordained by the elders and received an enabling gift to pastor and teach. He had neglected the gift,

which was necessary for him to serve. Twice, Paul tells him to stir the gift up.
- Every work of God is purposely built. We must take ownership of what God has placed in us. **Dedication produces excellence, and excellence leads to greater service in the kingdom.**
- The nature of being a living stone is growth: your gift can be expanded, shaped, and honed to excellence.

Our role in service encompasses our whole life.

There is a difference between serving and living a life of service.

The regulation of the gift
1 Timothy 4:15-16: "Be diligent in these matters; give yourself wholly to them, so that everyone may see your progress. Watch your life and doctrine closely. Persevere in them, because if you do, you will save both yourself and your hearers."

- Timothy had been given a ministry that was beyond his years. **Paul was teaching Timothy in chapters 4 and 5 the detailed procedure of how to use his gift to serve the different groups within the church.** It was vital that Timothy knew how to govern his gift so that his youth was not despised nor his ministry and service rejected. His service had to be comprehensive; he was to lead by example.
- The reason Paul takes such great pains in explaining how Timothy was to treat these various groups of people was so he could learn how to serve with his gift effectively in whatever situation he found himself.

In reality no one rises to prominence in his or her gift without the permission of God. God promotes from within His house.

The most practical test to measure how well you have used your gift in service is what I call the rocking chair test. When you are old, how will you respond to this question, "Am I proud of the way I served?" What will flash through your mind? When you serve in such a way that you will have no regrets, others will see God in you and your ministry.

Refining for service
1 Timothy 6:11: "But you, a man of God, flee from all this, and pursue righteousness, godliness, faith, love, endurance and gentleness."

- Paul does not call Timothy by name. Instead, he addresses him as

a man of God, reminding him that the basis of his service is the condition of his personal life.
- There is the outward pursuit of service, when you find and develop a gift and serve in a ministry. But those things have their roots in an inward pursuit. What we do must be driven by a strong devotional life. The standard for our service is set with our personal life, and for service to be lasting, it must have the substance of an authentic life behind it. Does this remind you of the covenant point "integrity"?

You Can Do It!
"God did not give us a spirit of timidity, but a spirit of power, of love and of self-discipline. So do not be ashamed to testify about our Lord" (2 Tim. 1:7-8).

There is Greatness on You!
"Guard the good deposit that was entrusted to you" (2 Tim. 1:14).

Expect Nothing But Success
"You...be strong in the grace that is in Christ Jesus" (2 Tim. 2:1).

Stay Committed To Your Purpose
"Do your best to present yourself to God as one approved, a workman who does not need to be ashamed" (2 Tim. 2:15).

Focus Your Energy
"Flee the evil desires of youth, and pursue righteousness" (2 Tim. 2:22).

Use Your Gift
"In the presence of God and of Christ Jesus, who will judge the living and the dead...I give you this charge" (2 Tim. 4:1).

Encourage Your Group: Actions for Group Study

1. Examine with one another how the gifts that you have been given need others' gifts to be used successfully.
2. Answer the question, "Is it possible to be pro-God but anti-church?"
3. Share some excuses you give for not using your gift as you could—disconnect, dodge, discount, devalue, or disassociate.
4. On a scale of one to ten, how would you rate your involvement in, and service for, God's house? (1 = Very Low; 10 = Very High.)
5. What theological hang-up do you have that clouds the call to serve?

> If your theology makes you spiritually impotent where you can no longer pass on faith to another person and you have no active role in building God's house, you have disqualified yourself.

Between You and God

1. If you could have one secret power, what would it be? Seek God's will in your life to discover if there is any gift that you have been given that's close to that.
2. Talk with God about whether you have ever done something that you felt has disqualified you from service.
3. If Christianity is pass/fail related to service, how are you doing?
4. Ask God to reveal to you how what you do helps build the house of God. Why is this important to God? To other students on your campus?
5. What would you do for God, if you knew it would work?
6. Who is your spiritual father or mother?
7. On a card, write Paul's six encouragements to Timothy. Spend time thinking about each one of them and visualize yourself using your gift with the strength of those encouragements.

> A life of service requires a successful melding of exquisite delicacy and astounding strength, flexibility and concentration. It demands the assembling of our gifts along with the grace to use them.

Dispossess to Possess: The Cycle of Purity

Dispossess to Possess: The Cycle of Purity

We all use fashion to attract others and to hide our flaws. Cool coverings have been a concern ever since Eve turned to Adam and said, "That fig leaf is so last season!"

Fashion now is an industry that preys on our securities, panders to our pride, and prevails through envy. We are in a constant state of panic because the fashion world tells us, "This is what you need to fit in—you'll be cool if you have this." But six months later they tell us, "You're a jerk if you have that—now you need this!"

Many are seduced to follow the trends, believing that if they wear a certain outfit they'll look like the fashion models strutting down the runway. Others refuse to follow and are forever stuck in the 70s—polyester pants, orange and lime green polka dot shirts and white wing tips—but lately, it's hard to tell if the person wearing that is a college student or a senior citizen.

Women struggle with fashion a great deal more than men. Men dress by smell—their whole wardrobe is sorted into two categories: dirty clothes that must be washed and dirty clothes that can be worn again. Men dress for one reason: protection from the elements. The closest a man gets to a makeover is buying a new car. The only reason men care about cars is that they know women love nice cars. If women loved cardboard, men would be cruising around in Frigidaire boxes.

But women have entire sections in stores dedicated to makeovers where, if you're not careful, even the men will be ambushed by professional sampler snipers. Cosmetic surgery is at an all-time high—it's possible to have every part of your body altered: calves, thighs, arms, cheek bones. There are people walking around with more plastic on them than a Corvette.

Fashion role models have been set in the houses of Gucci, Halston, Chanel, and Ralph Lauren. **We've forgotten that our Designer works for the house of God.** Gazing at ourselves in the mirror has become our favorite pastime. But we've forgotten to look into ourselves. Clothing, cosmetics, and constructive surgery all can help, but they will not bring us happiness, meaning, or fulfillment. That can only be found inside. It's a true statement: purity makes you more attractive because it manifests itself in all parts of your life. Purity is the world's only hope. It's only through a life of purity that we can transform the world.

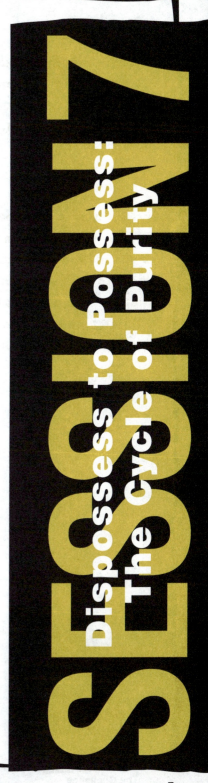

> It's a true statement: purity makes you more attractive because it manifests itself in all parts of your life.

> The purity that we already carry is our inspiration to live a life that provokes others to desire the purity that God has given us in Christ. A stained glass window of purity is what each of us is.

Purity is about how life is ordered. It's found in the ordinary choices of life—when you brush your teeth and how you eat a meal. Purity is not about obeying a handful of rules; it's about enjoying the fullness of life where the things of God can be experienced and demonstrated. Purity is not earned; it's granted to us at the moment of salvation. We're declared "pure" at the start. Earning a new status is not the focus. Conforming our life to God's present declaration of us is. The purity that we already carry is our inspiration to live a life that provokes others to desire the purity that God has given us in Christ. A stained glass window of purity is what each of us is. Our temptations, conflicts, and capabilities are themselves the fragile pieces in which the purity of Christ is seen.

Why is this such a struggle? Why is this so difficult? This stagnation partly comes from how we view purity, especially on the college campus. On your campus it's probable that purity is not a compliment—it's spoken of in condemning terms. "They're too good to be with us"; "goody two shoes"; "holier than thou." These are not labels we aspire to be known by, are they?

Another distortion of purity that must be avoided is legalism. Purity is the work of the heart. Reducing it to a set of rules trivializes the purpose of purity. Our hearts are no longer free when purity is distilled into custom. The danger of legalism is that it produces a feeling of attainment. It produces an unholy cockiness and cuts us off from the heart of God, which in turn forces us to deny who we are.

It's important to have a clear understanding of what purity is not, and what it is.

In our lives, God singles out an area to conform to His presence. In this cycle, we struggle, make mistakes, deal with issues, and the end result is that something is revealed, we are changed, and we move towards God's vision of us. The will of God is established. We struggle because, unknowingly, we are in a God-initiated cycle. We get caught somewhere and then quit. You must understand the stages of the cycle, identify where you are, cooperate with God, and at that point, move forward. Through the process, you'll discover something that has been there all along but has never been fully experienced. You'll discover that purity is not what you do; it's who you are in Christ.

The Cycle

This cycle is not something that I've made up—it's found in the life of Israel in the book of Judges. They turned away from God and got in trouble. God then sends judges to rescue them. But the problem was that they never got it. At any point, if they had understood who they were in the Lord, the demands He was placing on them, and what He had in store for them, then they could have broken out of the cycle. Instead of seeing the blessing of God come upon their lives, however, they cycle around and around and around. We do the same thing. We don't see the cycles God is taking us through, so instead of getting better, we just defend our place in the cycle. "I can stop any time I want."

Instead of just cycling down into disarray, we must move quickly to the design of God for our lives. The clearest sign that you're caught in the

You must understand the stages of the cycle, identify where you are, cooperate with God, and at that point, move forward. Through the process, you'll discover something that has been there all along but has never been fully experienced. You'll discover that purity is not what you do; it's who you are in Christ.

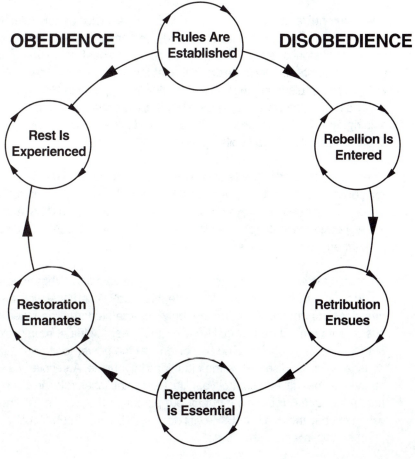

SESSION 7

cycle is that you experience progress for a period of time, the progress fades, and you're back to where you started. Relapsing in the cycle—nailing it down—can be found in making the changes God wants you to make. If you don't, then life will deteriorate into further anarchy.

Each stage is its own cycle. They're set in a descending line. Each stage gets worse and worse. In every stage, the way out is the will of God.

CYCLE 1: RULES ARE ESTABLISHED

In Judges 2, the cycle begins. "The Angel of the Lord went up from Gilgal to Bokim and said, 'I brought you up out of Egypt and led you into the land that I swore to give to your forefathers. I said, "I will never break my covenant with you, and you shall not make a covenant with the people of this land, but you shall break down their altars"'" (Judg. 2:1-2).

The moment He sends them into the land, He establishes this rule: "Kill everybody." (Don't take this out of context—remember we're talking about a specific historical event. This isn't a little voice speaking to you in the back of your hand.) God's desire was that they not entangle themselves with these people in any way. God was building a purity in His people, a purity out of which would come the Messiah. Israel was to be a bright and shining light to the nations. If they did not destroy their enemies, they could not be all that God called them to be.

The principle of the rule is this: You cannot possess what God has for you if you do not dispossess what is in the way. The will of God takes work. It doesn't always come without a struggle. You still have to do the work and make the choices to drive out the evil. It doesn't just disappear when we hit our knees and pray a little prayer.

What is in the way of the will of God for purity in your life? What needs to be driven out before God can dominate this area? When I ask you these questions, do not think you are the "only" college student giving the type answers you might be giving. However, the "deep" spiritual requirement of this principle is choice. God has given you the power to choose righteousness and to dispossess the old things in your life. A secular view of purity does not have to control your life. God establishes rules in our lives not to fine tune our behavior but for our person—who we are. The motivation to obey the rule is not, "Hey if I do this, I'll be pure," but, "I'm already pure, so this is what I should do."

CYCLE 2: REBELLION IS ENTERED

Verse 2 continues, "Yet you have disobeyed me. Why have you done this?" Verse 10 continues, "After that whole generation had been gathered to their fathers, another generation grew up, who knew neither the Lord nor what he had done for Israel." Verse 11: "Then the Israelites did evil in the eyes of the Lord…" Verse 12: "They forsook the Lord, the God of their fathers, who had brought them out of Egypt. They followed and worshiped various gods of the people around them."

They did whatever seemed right in their own eyes. Rebellion is caused by our casual view of the will of God. We end up flirting with danger morally and ethically, believing we can go unharmed. We think, "Hey what does it matter?" The will of God is for His people to fulfill. We must understand who we are. **Purity is not a law—it comes out of an understanding of who you are.**

To the point that a Christian does not know who he is in the Lord, he will rebel against the desires of God, not because he doesn't understand the law—the right way—but because of the way he sees himself and the character of God.

Some students believe that their sins are forgiven but not that their nature is changed. During the old covenant, the priest would sprinkle blood to cover the mercy seat so that God could not see the broken commandments—they were covered by the blood. In the new covenant, **Jesus is our sin magnet.** He died in our place. So in the old covenant, sins were covered. In the new covenant, sins are removed. We are given a new nature. A person goes to heaven not only because his sins are forgiven but also because his nature has been changed.

We have a new identity in Christ, and until we believe that, we will continue to rebel.
The new covenant reality is that you're a whole new person. Your nature is that you are a son or daughter of the Most High God. There is no way you can know who you are fully in the Lord and believe about yourself what God says about you, but then say, "I just don't know what to do about sex, pornography, and drugs."

Accepting Christ makes you a whole new person. The Bible speaks of us as a new nation and a new race, not defined by class or color but by the life of Christ. What does it mean to be a new race, to have this new nature?

Translation Graph

NEW COVENANT MESSAGE

You Are:
- Completely Level
- Totally Forgiven
- Fully Received
- God's Own Possession

TRANSLATES INTO

You Are:
- A Bad Person
- Unable To Live This Life
- Sinner Saved by Grace
- Not Worthy

> There is no way you can know who you are fully in the Lord and believe about yourself what God says about you, but then say, "I just don't know what to do about sex, pornography, and drugs."

Let's look at it in **two parts**: the content of the new race and the character of the new race. We'll look at some passages of Scripture so you can prove these truths for yourself.

Content of the new race

This is how God responds to his children in the new covenant: everything that He wants to see from us, He declares us to be.

- For the content of the new race, turn to 1 John 3:1. "How great is the love the Father has lavished on us, that we should be called children of God! And that is what we are." John writes this to show the difference between the old nature and the new nature.
- Your old nature died with Christ: "In the same way, count yourselves dead to sin but alive to God in Christ Jesus" (Rom. 6:11). Many of us believe that we are alive to God—we sing worship songs, read the Bible, and pray—but we refuse to believe that we are dead to sin. We refuse to accept that God has forgiven us.

So often college students struggle over one or two instances in their lives. They look back on the night they lost their virginity; drugs they did; an abortion they had—wishing that God would just take the guilt away. Well He has—by crucifying that person on the cross. Do you see it? The person who did those things is dead, and you either don't believe that God did that for you, or you think that if you just hadn't done that one thing, you would be right before God. But that's not an attitude of self-pity. It's self-righteousness. We must all admit that our whole lives are in rebellion against God, not just a handful of things that we did.

- But there comes a point when we have to forgive ourselves and walk in our new nature. That's why Paul writes, "In the same way count"—you must apply your new nature with God to every area of your life. You must respond to the new life within you.

- Second Corinthians 6:16 says, "I will dwell in them. I will walk among them. I will be their God. They will be my people" (NASB). *The life of God is within you. You carry with you the presence of God Himself.* Spiritually, you are pure in Christ!

Character of the new race
The character of the Christian is the life of the Spirit. As we learn to walk and worship, we show the fruits of the Spirit. We receive Christ as Lord, and we follow Him by the power of the Holy Spirit.
- Look at Romans 8:14-16: "Because those who are led by the Spirit of God are sons of God. For you did not receive a spirit that makes you a slave again to fear, but you have received the spirit of sonship. And by him we cry, 'Abba, Father!' The Spirit himself testifies with our spirit, that we are God's children."
- We are brought into a new family—the family of God. Everything that is His is ours. As He claimed a life of purity, that is ours to claim as well.

And it's a good thing that you now desire the things of God. As you can see from the list below, you have little time for sin. As His son you are…
- led by the Spirit (Rom. 8:14)
- serving the King aggressively (Matt. 4:10)
- glorifying God (Rom. 15:6)
- supporting righteousness (Rom. 6:12)
- opposing unrighteousness (Rom. 6:13)
- committed to global Christianization (Matt. 28:19)

If you doubt your role—and even if you don't—then look up these verses, read their contexts, and think about how your relationship with God opens up a whole new world of a life of purity.

CYCLE 3: RETRIBUTION ENSUES
"In his anger against Israel the Lord handed them over to raiders who plundered them"—what are the odds? "He sold

> *Do you see it? The person who did those things is dead, and you either don't believe that God did that for you, or you think that if you just hadn't done that one thing, you would be right before God. But that's not an attitude of self-pity. It's self-righteousness.*

> *As He claimed a life of purity, that is ours to claim as well.*

them to their enemies all around, whom they were no longer able to resist. Whenever Israel went out to fight, the hand of the Lord was against them to defeat them" (Judg. 2:14-15).

- Israel refused to get rid of the enemies, so God said, "Fine. They'll pick you apart. They'll plunder you and you'll be at war your whole life."
- Not seeing immediate consequences of our rebellion gives us the false confidence that we're getting away with it.
- Students get away from home, church, their youth group, and see everyone around them doing their own thing at college. So they say to themselves, "Nothing bad is happening to them—may as well try it out." Acts of impurity also draw holy consequences. Some scars never fade when we end up living away from God, dissatisfied with life.

CYCLE 4: REPENTANCE IS ESSENTIAL

"The Lord had compassion on them as they groaned under those who oppressed and afflicted them" (Judg. 2:18).

This is the message of the entire book of Judges: Repent. Repentance is allowing God to use you to make wise choices in terms of what you do and what you see. You are turning away from what you desire, to what God desires.

I do a number of CrossSeekers Covenant conferences. The outline I use when I speak is simple. The first session is the introduction to covenant faithfulness. In order to illustrate this idea, I use a big hula hoop as a symbol of the covenantal life. Stepping inside the hoop, I say, **"In covenant, good things happen."** Stepping out I say, **"Out of covenant, bad things happen."** This may sound simple, but it's true. Covenantal living is realizing that God has voluntarily bound Himself to His people. When they rebel, they suffer. When they repent, they're blessed. **Repentance means bringing every aspect of our lives into the circle.**

There is a God who has a will. Since we possess the nature of Christ, to do His will is not optional. If you think that nothing bad is happening to you because of your disobedience—so you think you're getting away with it—then let me tell you it's not true. **Never mistake God's patience for His permission.** No one gets away with anything.

God lets us go our own way; let's hope we come to our senses and turn around.

CYCLE 5: RESTORATION EMANATES

Verse 16: "Then the Lord raised up judges who saved them out of the hands of these raiders." Verse 18a: "Whenever the Lord raised up a judge for them, he was with the judge and saved them out of the hands of their enemies as long as the judge lived."

Restoration comes after repentance. This is not just the act of saying a little prayer so you can do it again.

We repent to be restored back to the will of God. In order for that happen, we must:

- Recognize the law is over.
- Understand who He is in us.
- Receive His life into that specific area.
- See that purity is no longer a big struggle—it's automatic.
- Live out the new commitment.

Then good things happen. Through this stage, God restores life where there used to be struggles. There is a cleansing, and purity begins to rise.

In this stage, everything that you've spiritually lost, God gives back to you.

That's incredibly motivating. We're energized with His design and desire for our lives.

CYCLE 6: REST IS EXPERIENCED

Judges 3:11: "Then the land had rest for forty years" (NASB).

They had truth rooted in their lives, understood who they were to God, and what they were to do. As long as they stayed in covenant and didn't return to idols, there was peace. Believing this truth keeps you pure. It's no coincidence that what brings impurity and heightens our sense of negative consequences, also brings a loss of peace. Stop disturbing the peace. Rest in your new nature. Live out of it. You don't have to go through these cycles every time in order to find rest.

Here's the tragedy to this story. Chapter 2 of Judges, verse 17, says, "They would not listen to their judges but prostituted themselves to other

> God lets us go our own way; let's hope we come to our senses and turn around.

> In this stage, everything that you've spiritually lost, God gives back to you.

gods," and verse 19 says, "the people returned to ways even more corrupt than those of their fathers." They never got it.

What happened was that they just kept cycling down deeper and deeper into despair. That's exactly what will happen to us without repentance and restoration of who we are. **In dispossessing the impurity in our lives, we will discontinue our downward spiral.**

Living the life of your new nature is an invitation to another level where purity is embraced, and it flows into the choices of your life.

Conclusion

I believe that everyone has a gap (and every mall does too). For a long time I struggled with knowing if I was making any progress in my spiritual life. My dad left when I was six, so I never had a man in my life to guide me in my spiritual walk. Even after being on the road speaking for the past eleven years, I still sometimes wonder how I can tell if I'm "getting it" spiritually. It's through that questioning that I discovered that our spiritual life can be measured by the time gap between God's conviction and our response to it.

Many times God convicts us of something, but we're slow to respond to it. We measure the gap in months and years, not hours and minutes. Many of us know what it is to feel the conviction of God in an area of life but to push it off.

There are many college students who have felt God say, "You need to get out of that relationship," and instead of following God's lead, they hold on, saying, "I'm not ready to let go." Many students regret not obeying God sooner. Maybe it's surrendering to God's call on your life for ministry. There are many people that feel the call of God on their lives but are running from it. Year after year they are putting off their obedience (which is a nice way of saying that they're just plain disobedient). This is not an act of covenantal purity.

And the time gap isn't only a measure of your general spiritual condition. **It also shows you exactly what God needs to work on.** Because wherever the gaps are, that's where God is dealing with us in our walks with Him. When thinking about specific issues, there are three types of gaps: instruction, instinct, and integrity. Let's look at each of these three in quick detail.

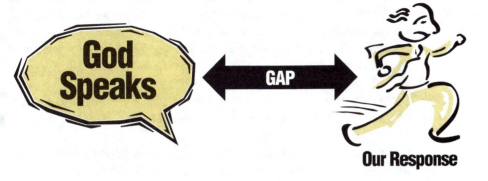

Obey the instructions.

"According to the foreknowledge of God the Father, through the sanctifying work of the Spirit, for obedience to Jesus Christ and sprinkling by his blood: Grace and peace be yours in abundance" (1 Pet. 1:2).

How well do we take the Word of God to heart? It's one thing to read it. It's one thing to write it in a notebook. It's another thing to have it written on your heart.

You may say that you're having deep quiet times, faithfully guarding the inerrancy of Scripture, and giving money to the Wycliffe Bible Translators, but unless you submit to all that is written in the Bible, you can't persuade me that you believe a single word of it.

Closing the gap in regard to obeying the Word of God means that you have to obey even when you don't want to—even if it goes against your cheap desire of the moment because you trust that acting on His instruction will bring you all you desire. The tragedy is that many college students would prefer to find pleasure in past injuries than find the great freedom and exhilarating joy that is ours if we follow His instruction.

Order your instincts.

"Do not grieve the Holy Spirit of God…Get rid of all bitterness, rage and anger, brawling and slander, along with every form of malice…Be kind and compassionate to one another, forgiving each other" (Eph. 4:30-32).

"There must not be even a hint of sexual immorality, or any kind of impurity, or of greed" (Eph. 5:3).

> How well do we take the Word of God to heart? It's one thing to read it. It's one thing to write it in a notebook. It's another thing to have it written on your heart.

We all struggle with our own drives and weaknesses—areas where we're easily taken in—but we narrow the gap by the choices we make. Closing the gap means feeling your spiritual instincts and starving your carnal ones. You don't have to date the antichrist; you don't have to drink; you don't have to smoke.

Controlling your instincts keeps you from indulging in the luxury of a wild emotion that will only leave you with a broken heart.

Closing the instinct gap means making appropriate boundaries given our weaknesses. Now that's not something we want to do: first, because we want to sin anyway—let's face it—and second, because we don't want to humble ourselves and say, "Well, I guess I'm not strong enough to resist that. I should just remove myself from that situation completely."

Obtain integrity.

"The integrity of the upright guides them, but the unfaithful are destroyed by their duplicity" (Prov. 11:3).

Integrity is about living in accordance with all that God has made us in Christ. In life's difficult moments, we want to say that our struggles come from uncertainty. "I don't know if we should be dating," for example. But far too often it's an issue of purity. We know what we should do, but we choose not to do it. That creates the integrity gap, and we know who suffers—we do. The anguish that we feel is not from uncertainty; it's from disobedience. We must take hold of—we must experience—purity. Refusing to do so will only cause us grief.

With regards to handling the issues of everyday life, there are only two choices: do it your own way, by doing whatever seems best, or do it God's way, by dealing with the situations so as not to grieve the Spirit of God in you or to hinder your usefulness to God. Purity, then, means choosing to do life God's way in the major areas as well as in the minor ones.

Purity is when your whole being is transformed by and empowered by the Holy Spirit. When you are pure, all that God wants you to do comes naturally to you—so you respond quickly because His way pleases you. His way is who you are.

Encourage Your Group: Actions for Group Study

1. Answer this question: "Can God forgive your sin without changing your nature?"
2. Give examples with other students of how specific sin in one area can result in increased irritation or sorrow in a totally different part of life. (For example, when you criticize someone for being sexually active, is that righteousness speaking, or is it covetousness?)
3. If you are not living a life of covenantal purity, are you happy? How can you know happiness?
4. Do you believe that acts of impurity draw holy consequences? If yes, then how?
5. Ask, "Is peace the absence of conflict, or is it something greater?"
6. Matthew 5:8 says that the pure in heart will see God. How can this verse serve as a summary of our study on purity? (Be specific.)

Between You and God

1. Pray for help in dealing with what needs to be driven out of your life so that you can take hold of what God has for you.
2. Seek to understand in your relationship with Christ why God restores us.
3. First Peter 3 speaks of repenting and doing good. Ask God to help you understand in practical ways, what role doing good plays in repentance.
4. Ask God to reveal to you where the gaps need to be closed in your life.
5. What do the gaps in your life say about your progress toward purity in Christ?

> With regards to handling the issues of everyday life, there are only two choices: do it your own way, by doing whatever seems best, or do it God's way, by dealing with the situations so as not to grieve the Spirit of God in you or to hinder your usefulness to God.

No More Tears: The Power of Covenant Friendship

No More Tears: The Power of Covenant Friendship

Friendships have always been important. When we were younger, it was easy to pick friends. Our only criterion was whoever said, "Hi" to us first. Those were the days when we could pass out valentines to the whole class without being considered weird.

Acceptance is still the major test in establishing friendships. If they like us and seem cool, we think we've found a friend. But that's not always fail-safe.

Our need for relationships is fierce. We need friends. Research shows that they make us healthier—unless you're drinking out of the same glass. Friends accept us, instill confidence, and give us courage to do things we wouldn't ordinarily do, like try out for a sport, ask someone out on a date, or drink a six pack of Scope.

The increase of the Internet has heightened the loss of relationship skills; it has become apparent for many of us who use the Internet as our primary mode of communication that it's harder for us to open up to other people than to open a children's medicine bottle.

In this high-tech age, when so many people are floating alone in cyberspace, we need to be reminded that friendships are both important and necessary. There is still the need for connectedness. Some people settle for facsimile friendships by developing cyber-friendships. People bond in chat rooms. They have important conversations like, "I like green—what's your favorite color?"—or intellectually stimulating debates like, "Is orange a color?"

This generation thirsts for a spiritual reality in relationships. Christians relate in marginally spiritual ways. Some students talk about the pastor's sermon like they would his tie. Often, there's neither power nor conviction in our conversations, and we are not challenged to move beyond that level.

Most collegians live, longing for meaningful relationships but are really just looking after themselves, because they believe that the world can satisfy their needs. We are vaguely aware that there is a higher dimension to friendship that could make us happier.

But, as Christian college students, we can take refuge in all that the new covenant has brought us: **the abolition of sins, assurance of salvation, and the activity of the Spirit.** This last element of the new covenant is relational. The Spirit of God lives in us. This is how we can speak about Christ being with us—the Spirit gives us access through Christ to God Himself. The Spirit also enables us to relate to each other.

Covenant brings a new **safety**. It's easier to relate to others when the fear of rejection has been eliminated. A new **vision** helps us begin to see God at work in our relationships. A new **wisdom** helps us learn to accept others, as well as the design of others. A new **power** comes, as the Holy Spirit produces in us the ability to trust others and be trusted by others. We begin to hold back our criticism, accepting people as they are and trusting that God will work in them, just as He is working in us.

Everything we wish to find in relationships with others, all the things we want others to be to us, and our greatest desires for healthy relationships are found in living the new covenant. The new covenant energizes every relationship that we have.

Being a better listener, affirming others, learning to adjust, and finding relief from conflict are all about self-improvement—God is not a necessary part of the equation for these things to happen. How does the Spirit invade our relationships? What does covenant look like? What does it require of us?

God has created friendship and desires that we adapt to His standards. When we do so, friendship is experienced at such a level and depth that nothing can compare to it. To allow friendships to function the way they should function, we must seek a new understanding and adjust to a new approach on our part. **There are three aspects to understanding how the dimension of the covenant affects our relationships:** learn the role; be led by the rationale; and live in response to the covenant. Let me share with you how each works.

1) Learn the role

"Let's just be friends." These words have stung the hearts of many men and women, and even now as you read this, you may be having flashbacks.

As powerful as that memory may be, it demonstrates what we all know

> The increase of the Internet has heightened the loss of relationship skills; it has become apparent for many of us who use the Internet as our primary mode of communication that it's harder for us to open up to other people than to open a children's medicine bottle.

> A new power comes, as the Holy Spirit produces in us the ability to trust others and be trusted by others.

about relationships—we place people in different categories. Not all friendships are equal. Every girl I know can distinguish relationships by emphasizing the same word differently: "Well, I like him, but I don't *like* him." For guys, it's different—we say, "I spent money. *Money.*" Regardless, we all recognize that we characterize relationships differently—here's my best attempt.

Acquaintances
These are the people that enter our lives randomly, like the guy with the dreadlocks, orange sunglasses, tie-dyed t-shirt, and red jeans who is in your world literature class. You see him one day in the cafeteria. So you interrupt someone telling you about the biological differences between shrimp and prawns to say, "Hey, that one guy there is in my lit. class." You don't know his name, and you have no real commitment to him.

Associates
Specific activities bring you into contact with associates. These are the people on your team, theater group, band, etc. They are in your

Arenas of Friendship

life because you share a **common interest**, and the majority of the time you see them in the context of that activity.

Accountability

Close friends, best friends, and perhaps brothers and sisters fall into this category. They exert **incredible influence** in the recesses of your life because they have access to your heart. There is acceptance, encouragement, and constructive involvement. These are the people you take along with you.

Allies

A covenant friendship is in its own category. This is not another form of accountability. There is an element of accountability there, but that's not what the friendship is about. It goes deeper than that. The question that must be asked is, "Is this a biblical model?" Does the Bible make a case for covenant friendship? It would be easy to think, "Why would I need that in my life?"

A covenant friend is an ally who is committed to the design of God for your life. In our lives, there need to be mentors, pastors, and best friends. There must also be covenant friends.

We can see in Scripture that what happened between Jonathan and David impacted David's role with his family, his government, and his army. Jonathan helped David become an instrument of God.

Likewise, without a covenant friend, you are not an instrument. You are a target.

Throughout Scripture, this covenantal type of friendship is clearly seen. God placed them in Scripture to show us the necessary and pivotal role they play in our lives. Look at the following examples.

Naomi and Ruth

Ruth, in the midst of extreme change and the loss of security, says, "Where you go, I will go." That's what is normally said in a marriage ceremony, but Ruth says it to her mother-in-law. **It's a friendship that goes deeper than common interests or a relationship through marriage.** After all, any married person can tell you how difficult that would be to say to an in-law. In fact, most couples think that a pleasure cruise is driving the in-laws to the airport.

Moses and Aaron
Sensing at the same time his own weakness as well as the greatness of his task as a deliverer of the people, Moses finds his mouthpiece in Aaron. Aaron accepts his role, but in doing so, he sacrifices his own comfort and safety. **One of the marks of covenant friendship is a deep acceptance of the other person's gifts and a willingness to help the other person fulfill his or her God-given purpose.**

Joshua and Caleb
Men with a different spirit, they sensed the design and the resources of God while negativity and despair spread throughout Israel. In faithfulness to each other and to God, they spoke out boldly, in spite of the opposition. **Covenant friends support each other to be courageous and to stand for Christ regardless of the situation—good or bad.**

Elijah and Elisha
Four times Elisha says to Elijah, "I will not leave you." It is out of this relationship that Elisha receives a double portion of power—he performed twice as many miracles as Elijah. We become like those we spend time with. Elisha learned how to fulfill his role as a prophet through his fellowship with Elijah, and **covenant friendships today inspire sincerity and infuse power into our lives and our devotions.**

Paul and Timothy
From the beginning, Paul had seen the gift that Timothy carried. Again and again, Paul stood up for Timothy when his youthfulness caused others to question his ministry. What Paul instilled, Timothy played out through his whole life. Covenant friends are more than mentors. They're not there to maximize your potential. **They're there to fan into flame the God-things in our lives.** A covenant friend will affirm and build by bringing penetrating wisdom into every area of our lives.

Paul and Onesimus
In a little-read letter of Paul, we read about Paul's tender concern for the slave Onesimus. Writing to Philemon, Paul says that he is sending Onesimus, "my very heart," in the hopes that Philemon will be persuaded to give Onesimus his freedom. This kindred spirit that Paul has with Onesimus characterizes the unique spirit of covenant

friendships. Paul writes, "So if you consider me a partner, welcome him as you would welcome me. If he has done you any wrong, or owes you anything, charge it to me" (Philem. 17-18). Covenant friends aren't the ones who will accuse you in public for some wrong you may or may not have done. **They're the ones who will take the hit for you and stand by you when you do wrong.**

Covenant friends are important. They can best be defined as extraordinary people. Their roles are not limited to accountability, mentoring, or pastoring. Though those are important roles, they are not necessarily elements of a covenant relationship.

2) Led by the rationale

"Why can't everyone be like me?" That statement is the surest way to set yourself up for trouble. The greatest barrier to covenantal friendship is selfishness. Thinking we deserve more than others is never a healthy way of developing relationships. Instead, it's a guaranteed path to isolation and loneliness. "What's in it for me?" is an anti-relational approach that creates the feeling of rejection in others. People will start thinking that you don't care about them; you just care about what they can do for you.

Christians in relationships can be the biggest hypocrites. You might think the message of the unconditional love and forgiveness of Christ can be shared with an unbelieving world, but still refuse to exhibit that love and forgiveness to other Christian brothers and sisters. Most people's friendships aren't any stronger spiritually because of their propensity for selfishness.

Before we examine what friendship is, look at the margin for advice on how to lose the friends you've got—if that's what you want to do.

Now let's look at the source for true friendship by looking at God's friendship with us. Jesus defined this relationship in John 15:12 when He said, "Love each other as I have loved you." He loved them covenantally. When Jesus chose the twelve, He was aware of their potential and their shortcomings. James and John were ambitious. They each tried to promote themselves before Christ. Peter was impetuous, often shooting his mouth off, making promises he could not fulfill. For Matthew, it was materialism.

Instead of being judgmental, He involved Himself in their lives. He

---

The rationale of covenant is love. God moves towards us in love. It's what God does, and it's what we should carry out into all other relationships.

How to Lose Your Friends…

- Become stingy with your life.
- Never open up.
- Talk about yourself all the time.
- Always have something negative to say.
- Make your friends feel like they're just a small part of your plan for world domination.

came to their jobs, to their homes; He knew their families. They saw Jesus take an interest in their lives. They soon would come to see who He was and understand His message.

These men did more than watch. They followed Him and became associated with Him. Jesus made their lives His focus.

Jesus modeled covenant love with His life. He made their interest His interest. His actions said, "I'm interested in what's best for you."

What do people hear you saying by the way you treat people? Covenant love is sacrificial. It's going to cost you something that is real to you. If it didn't, it wouldn't be a sacrifice.

Jesus' love was not restricted to the social elite. Jesus offered His friendship to the poor and the weak; the disconnected and the lonely; the homeless and the clueless. Years after Jesus' death, Paul writes, "While we were still sinners, Christ died for us" (Rom. 5:8).

How far are we to take this covenant thing? Jesus took it all the way to the cross. That was the ultimate demonstration of covenant fellowship to the world. He made our interest His interest, and He took it all the way to the cross.

Others first? Yes. This is the covenant mission of Philippians 2:3: "Do nothing out of selfish ambition or vain conceit…consider others better than yourselves." This is quite staggering when you think that Jesus Himself did just that for us. He set aside His glory and His status and, for us, He lived under the same restrictions that we do. He was consistent in His pursuit: it was His happiness to labor for our happiness. And He carried it through from the cradle to the cross.

> **Think of how God has treated you in Christ:**
> • He became sin for you.
> • He moved into a relationship with you.
> • He loved you unconditionally.
> • He didn't judge you.

Now let us extend the same treatment to others on the campus. He stayed, even when we rebelled. He forgave at the moment of our return.

Loving as He loved us requires that we step into other students' lives and love students who we'd have no reason to love. Our response is not determined by other people's character, morality, or the sensitivity they show in their dealings with us. That's not the issue. But you extending the love of Christ is.

3) Live in response
A covenant biography
- Jonathan had it made. He was the most eligible bachelor in the entire kingdom of Israel.
- Everything in his life—from school to friendships to what he could and could not do—was focused on the knowledge that he was going to be king of Israel.
- He would have his place in history. The sovereign nation that the Lord Himself had established for His people would be his kingdom.
- One day, standing on the hillside with his father, all of that changed. Looking down, Jonathan noticed the army of Israel camped across the valley from the Philistines, their archenemies.
- Jonathan watched a little shepherd boy named David, about his age, walk into the valley and kill Goliath. Goliath was enormous—ten feet tall with a spear the size of a beam—but David killed him with a sling.
- Then Jonathan heard a rumor about David, and he must have wondered if it was true. People said that when David was young the prophet Samuel broke open oil and poured it on his head, saying, "God has removed His hand from Saul, and David, you are going to be the next king of Israel."
- Jonathan should have been jealous, bitter and angry. He had good reason to hate, fear and resent David. The single purpose for which Jonathan had been groomed—to be king—had been taken from him by David.
- I'm sure Jonathan hurt deeply, but that did not determine his response. There was something deeper driving his will. What did he know that we need to know?

The power of covenant friendship is seen in two parts.

A) SUBMIT YOUR LIFE TO ANOTHER COVENANT PERSON (1 SAM. 18:3-4)

There was no question in Jonathan's mind that God intended for David to be king. Jonathan's actions spoke louder than any words contained here. He removed his clothes of royalty and placed them on David.

Jonathan pledged himself to help David in fulfilling God's decree, and, by giving him his sword, belt, and bow, he showed that he would help him by being his servant—not his king (1 Sam. 18:4).

You are an important part of God's plan in someone else's life. Someone needs what you have to offer. But the cause of submission isn't duty, obligation, accountability, or resources—it's love. Jonathan loved David as himself.

The majority of our best friendships take time to develop. They grow in seasons and stages. This is not always the case with covenant friendships. They are in a moment of time. It seems that Jonathan and David haven't ever been together. But it feels like they've been lifelong friends.

IMPERATIVES
The challenge is to find a covenant friend and enter into such a role. The temptation is to make a list and to launch out on a hunt to find that person. But covenant friendships aren't manufactured out of human ingenuity. God brings us together—there must be the smack of God on it.

INGREDIENTS
Take a moment to write your own description of good friendship, using the following key words. Remember to use all the words. Try to do it in the margin, and be prepared to share your description with others.

Character-driven
Open
Vision
Empowers
Navigates
Assesses
Networks
Truthful

IMPACT
In covenant friendship, even as we look out for the person, God uses them to bless us, too.

Covenant Friendships

1. Protect you.
2. Help you become a person of character.
3. Keep you on track.
4. Hold you back from the things that will destroy you.

Look at Jonathan. He did what was right, and he had a terrible role model: Saul, the fallen king.

Saul: A Non-covenantal response

Turn to 1 Samuel 20:30-31 to see Saul's approach. Saul is angry because he has learned that Jonathan has been speaking with David, whom Saul considers an enemy. He screams, "You son of a perverse and rebellious woman!" (That's right—you know how we'd say that today. Everything's in the Bible.) "You son of a perverse and rebellious woman! Don't I know that you have sided with the son of Jesse to your own shame and to the shame of the mother who bore you? As long as the son of Jesse lives on this earth, neither you nor your kingdom will be established. Now send and bring him to me, for he must die!"

Saul says, "Do you realize that if David lives, we'll lose the kingdom? You won't be king. David will take what is rightly yours. His death is the only way to protect your throne." Saul sees everything he has lived for being ripped out of his hands by an upstart shepherd who knows how to play the harp. He cannot understand why his son would be devoted to David, instead of feeling hatred toward him, as he does.

Saul died an angry, bitter, and crazy man, because he spent his whole life trying to resist the desire of God.

Once again, what makes Jonathan so different from Saul? What in the world does Jonathan know that we don't know? Take a moment and jot down your thoughts. _____
_____
_____
_____
_____
_____
_____
_____
_____

In spite of how he felt, Jonathan responded covenantally.

B) Support the Prerogative of God

The answer is found in 1 Samuel 20:13. Jonathan, speaking to David, says, "But if my father is inclined to harm you, may the Lord deal with me, be it ever so severely, if I do not let you know and send you away safely." He says, "Even if my dad comes after you, I promise that I am going to protect you in every way that I can." He also says, "May the Lord be with you, as he has been with my father." **Jonathan blessed David because he recognized God's choice and submitted to it.** God had chosen David as the king. Jonathan recognized that it was God's will. Jonathan had two choices—to submit himself to God's decision or to defy God. Jonathan submitted and worked towards fulfilling God's desire. He devoted himself to David, not because David deserved to be the king but because the sovereign God Himself had made a choice.

Would you call this covenantal living? Check one. ❏ Yes ❏ No
Why did you answer as you did?

Jonathan could have thrown a fit. He could've looked at David and said, "I'm supposed to be king—not him." "He knows nothing of ruling. He's just a common worker from the wrong family. He hasn't been trained in things, as I have—how dare he try to take my place." But instead, he looked to God and accepted the prerogative of God. He asked the question, "How should the king's son respond to what God is doing? How should the king's son, with his knowledge of political affairs and access to the highest powers in the land act in the face of God's sovereign choice?" He didn't ask, "How should the king's son respond when someone tries to take his place?" but "How should the king's son respond when God has chosen someone else to be king?"

"But I want to be king!" Pride and selfishness are a subtle enemies.They manifest themselves in the form of jealousy or resentment. We speak in terms of getting our feelings hurt, of being angry or hurt. But we don't speak of being proud. Too often we can't be happy for someone else's success because, we are territorial and their success becomes our failure. So it becomes impossible for us to be with people, because they threaten our world.

Jonathan died in an obscure place, in an obscure battle that amounted to nothing, but he died having surrendered himself to God's choice that David would be king. What Jonathan discovered was that David was not going to be king because of his superior talent or skill.

> Jonathan submitted and worked towards fulfilling God's desire. He devoted himself to David, not because David deserved to be the king but because the sovereign God Himself had made a choice.

> **What Jonathan discovered was that David was not going to be king because of his superior talent or skill. David was going to be king because it was God's prerogative. And Jonathan had confidence in God's character.**

David was going to be king because it was God's prerogative. **And Jonathan had confidence in God's character.** He trusted that God—a loving, all-knowing, and all-present being—was ordering his steps. So even when he died, his death made sense. He didn't think, "If I die, who will rule God's people?" He already knew the answer—David would.

Jonathan and Saul both had the same end—death on the battlefield—but their lives were totally different. I don't have to persuade whose life was better. Jonathan died at peace, having lived in covenant. Saul died at war with David, Jonathan, and God, never having had rest since he rejected God and God's prerogative.

Jonathan understood three things that helped him support the prerogative of God.

1) God has made each person unique.

God has made you with your own blend of talents and skills. God has made some people richer and some people poorer. He has made some people talented in many areas and others talented in a few. You can't just be anyone. I'll never be a rock star. I'll never be a movie star. I'll never play professional basketball. I won't be president of the United States. I wasn't made to be any of those things. I was made to write books, travel the country, and tell people that God loves them. That's what I was made to do.

2) God has given us unique freedom to choose.

But in addition to giving you certain talents that are unique to you, He has also given you freedom. And people exercise their freedom in many ways, don't they? People help me, hurt me, threaten me, encourage me, and discourage me. Hopefully some people out there ("Hi, mom!") even love me.

3) God has a unique destiny.

God's behind it all. Even when people hurt us and make choices that affect us in a negative way, He's in control of it. That's how powerful our God is. That's the mystery of the cross—non-covenantal men crucified the covenant man out of jealousy and anger—and God has used that to save us. The covenantal response is, **"God, nothing comes into** my life that you don't allow." If we have that approach, we'll be free to love our enemies, and the power of God will be released in our lives. We will love people that aren't lovable, even when they're not acting just as we want them to act, because we will trust that, at the end of our lives, we will have accomplished all that God wanted us to accomplish—even if the bitter people around us labored to stop us from doing what God had set out for us. From this understanding comes the security to live covenantally towards others. **God will do the fighting for you.**

Now the choice is ours. We can support those around us to fulfill God's purposes in this world, or we can break apart trying to shake God into submission. (A word to the dense—the second option just won't work.) You must ask yourself, as Jonathan did, "In light of God's prerogative, how should I respond to this situation?" Because of my confidence in God, can I support what He's doing in my life and in the lives of others?

C) SERVE PROACTIVELY

Jonathan models the heart of covenantal friendship by how he interacts with David in 1 Samuel 20.

THEY INVITE; THEY DON'T INVADE

"'Come,' Jonathan said, 'let's go out into the field.' So they went there together" (1 Sam. 20:11).

Jonathan knew his father all too well. He also knew that David was in a crisis and that Saul, his father, had something to do with it. Jonathan takes David to a place where he could talk privately.

A safe person, a covenantal friend, is someone who invites. They invite conversation; they invite relationship. But they don't invade personal space. Covenantal friendship has an element of courtship: it is purposeful and faithful but never overbearing. Covenantal friends invite; they don't invade.

Going "out into the field" must have been the ancient equivalent of going out for a coffee or going to the mall. Jonathan understands the need for secrecy and the importance of intimacy. Friendship is always an invitation. It doesn't say, "Do this for me" or, "Here's how you fit into my life." Covenantal friendship says, like Jonathan, "Come,

> **A safe person, a covenantal friend, is someone who invites.**

and let us"—let us go, let us live, let us cry, and let us laugh. But in everything, let us be together. They invite; they don't invade.

THEY QUESTION; THEY DON'T ACCUSE

"'Never!' Jonathan replied. 'You are not going to die! Look, my father doesn't do anything great or small without confiding in me. Why would he hide this from me? It's not so!'" (1 Sam. 20:2).

Jonathan wasn't completely aware of what was going on, although he suspected something. Even though David was blaming Jonathan, he didn't get defensive. David was on the run, and he asked Jonathan if he'd done anything wrong. He was questioning—he didn't accuse. Even more surprising is Jonathan's similar approach. I would've said, "Well, of course you have. You've turned the people's hearts to yourself, away from my dad, and you'll steal the throne away from me, his son." But that's not Jonathan's response. He answers David's question with a question, but he's not trying to be clever or secretive. He honestly doesn't know. But for David, he will find out.

So often arguments break out between friends because we don't know all of the facts and we're too impatient to learn them. We want to ride into town with both guns blazing, not even waiting for the dust to settle. But that's not friendship. Friends question; they don't accuse.

THEY TELL THE TRUTH; THEY DON'T DENY

"'Never!' Jonathan said. 'If I had the least inkling that my father was determined to harm you, wouldn't I tell you?'" (1 Sam. 20:9).

David's tone intensified. He was under stress. But Jonathan took no offense. He stayed committed to do the right thing, even though it was going to cost him dearly. And so Jonathan becomes a traitor to his father and to his own hope for being king. Here he is, before his eyes, siding with David rather than the king, his own father. And Jonathan is willing to tell the truth, the hard truth. We feel uncomfortable saying that we don't like someone's new shoes. Jonathan was willing to say, "My dad wants you dead." Now that's telling the truth.

And that's a quality of friendship that many of us don't have. We're not willing to be honest with people. We do not expect or demand it. If I say, "Do you like this shirt?" that's not what I'm saying at all, is it? I'm saying, "Hey, you haven't noticed my new shirt yet, and I want you to compliment me on it." A girl says to her friend, "I went out with John last night; isn't he great?" She doesn't want to hear, "No, he's the antichrist. Stay away from him. He'll ruin your walk with God." But we must tell the hard truth when it is truth to do so. Covenant friends tell the truth; they don't deny.

THEY RESPOND; THEY DON'T RUN AWAY

"Jonathan said to David, 'Whatever you want me to do, I'll do for you'" (1 Sam. 20:4).

Jonathan knew that David was in trouble and needed help. He understood God's plan for David's future, so he responded to help him. Jonathan didn't abandon David in his time of need. On the contrary, when David was alone and on the run, Jonathan was there for him. And he didn't step in and say, "I'll stick around, but you better play by my rules." No! He said, "Tell me what to do. I'm willing to help."

You may be ashamed of your checkered past, embarrassed to tell your Christian friends about the drugs you've done, the people you've slept with, or the booze you've chugged in the places where you passed out. You shouldn't be. Christ took that shame from you and bore it on the cross. What's really embarrassing, what really angers me, is the friend who calls himself your Christian friend but runs away from you at the point of your need or at the time of a confession. **If that's your friend's response, then you need a better friend.** And if you're the so-called friend who has run away, then shame on you. You're no friend. Friends respond; they don't run away.

THEY PROTECT; THEY DON'T EXPOSE

"And Jonathan had David reaffirm his oath out of love for him, because he loved him as he loved himself" (1 Sam. 20:17).

Something stronger than Jonathan's family association was working in him. We learn what motivated Jonathan to protect David: love. He could have exposed David. He would have been honored by his father for doing so. **But Jonathan loved David with his life**, and he sensed God's purpose in David's life. Not only did he protect David, but he also blessed him, saying in verse 13, "May the Lord be with

> We learn what motivated Jonathan to protect David: love. He could have exposed David. He would have been honored by his father for doing so. But Jonathan loved David with his life, and he sensed God's purpose in David's life. Not only did he protect David, but he also blessed him, saying in verse 13, "May the Lord be with you as He has been with my father." Jonathan protected; he did not expose.

you as He has been with my father." Jonathan protected; he did not expose.

You may think, "Well that's easy; I'm not that kind of friend," but let's face it, you're not. You've either never been in that situation—"Next time yer friend Bill comes over again, I'm gonna blow his ear off fer what he said about yo' Mamma"—or you've let your friend take the hit—holding his hangups and personal problems in the spotlight so people don't notice yours. But that's not friendship. Friends protect; they don't expose.

Encourage Your Group: Actions for Group Study

1. James Carville wrote a book to defend his loyalty to Bill Clinton, entitled *Stickin' the Case for Loyalty*. Discuss what your response should be if someone you've known for a long time does something terrible.
2. Examine and share how supporting the prerogative of God can keep you from being hurt in any relationship.
3. Think: is it more difficult for you to tell someone that he's doing something wrong, or is it more difficult for you to keep from telling someone that he's doing something wrong? Be prepared to share your thoughts with the group.
4. Would you describe your friendship style like Genghis Khan or the Pillsbury Dough Boy?
5. When Jesus says, "Love each other as I have loved you," we often think of the crucifixion. But Jesus said these words before the crucifixion, so his disciples must have been thinking of something else when He said them. What do you think characterized Jesus' friendship with His disciples? How did He treat them?

Between You and God

1. Is it difficult or easy to find a covenant friend? Discuss this with God.
2. Has there ever been a time when you've put someone else first?
3. How important is it to have someone who considers you a covenant friend?
4. How does a covenantal friendship influence all of your other relationships?
5. How is a covenant friend more important than an accountability partner?

6. How should the principles of covenant friendship (invite, don't invade; question, don't accuse; etc.) impact our other relationships (acquaintances, associates, etc.)?
7. How did the covenant friends listed in this chapter influence their relationships with others?

The Challenge

I hope you better understand covenant living and how it can transform your own personal world. Once our lives are in the proper relationship with Christ, we can accept "The Challenge." Within the CrossSeekers Covenant we read these words, "I accept the challenge to divine daring, to consecrated recklessness for Christ, to devout adventure in the face of ridiculing contemporaries. I acknowledge I am created in the image of God and am committed to excellence as a disciple of Jesus Christ."

Join thousands of other college students whose lives are about "The Challenge."

As you join us on the journey to be a CrossSeeker, in the next few pages you will see additional resources designed within the CrossSeekers program to assist you in your growth. Let me encourage you to examine these for both personal and group Bible study in future days.

CrossSeekers Resources

CrossSeekers: Discipleship Covenant for a New Generation
by Henry Blackaby and Richard Blackaby

Discover the six CrossSeekers principles brought to life in a user-friendly, practical, story-telling format. This study sets the stage for an exploration of each CrossSeekers Covenant point. Biblical and contemporary examples of promises made, promises kept, and promises broken, along with consequences, bring the biblical truths home to today's college students.
• 9 sessions • Interactive in format • Leader's helps included • $8.95
ISBN 0-7673-9084-9

CrossSeekers: Transparent Living, Living a Life of Integrity
by Rod Handley

Integrity. Everyone talks about it. God *delights* in it. We *demand* it. But what exactly *is* integrity, and is it important? If you want to be a person of integrity, to live the kind of life Christ modeled—to speak the truth in love, to stand firm in your convictions, to be honest and trustworthy, then *Transparent Living, Living a Life of Integrity* is for you! This study supports the CrossSeekers Covenant principle *integrity.*
• 6 sessions • Leader's guide included • $6.95
ISBN 0-7673-9296-5

CrossSeekers: Holy and Acceptable, Building a Pure Temple
by Dave Edwards

First Corinthians 6 tells us that our bodies are temples of the Holy Spirit. But what does that mean, and why should we care? This study looks at what it means for us to be God's temple. Through Bible study and contemporary situations, the physical, mental, and spiritual aspects are explored, along with their interrelatedness, as well as what to do when you fail in your pursuit of purity. This study supports the CrossSeekers Covenant principle *purity.*
• 6 sessions • Interactive in format • Leader's guide included • $6.95
ISBN 0-7673-9428-3

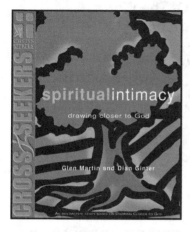

CrossSeekers: Spiritual Intimacy, Drawing Closer to God
by Glen Martin and Dian Ginter
Spiritual Intimacy will intensify the desire of your heart to know God more intimately, help you realize where you are in the process of drawing closer to God, and show you how to move ahead by knowing God on six successive levels. This study supports the CrossSeekers covenant point *spiritual growth*.
• 6 sessions • Interactive in format • Leader's guide included • $6.95
ISBN 0-7673-9427-5

CrossSeekers: Fearless, Sharing an Authentic Witness
by William Fay and Dean Finley
Fearless, Sharing an Authentic Witness equips collegians for sharing their faith with others. Sessions address concepts such as our lives as a living witness (using the CrossSeekers Covenant points for discussion), how Jesus shared with persons He met, learning where God is at work in another person's life, a threat-free and effective method for presenting the gospel, and addressing difficult questions/situations. Based on *Share Jesus Without Fear*, this study supports the CrossSeekers Covenant principle *witness*.
♦ 6 sessions ♦ Interactive in format
♦ Leader's guide included ♦ $6.95
ISBN 0-7673-9865-3

CrossSeekers: The Highest Education, Becoming a Godly Man
by Gregg Matte
Authored by the highly effective collegiate speaker, Gregg Matte, this CrossSeekers resource helps guide college men toward a lifestyle of Covenant living by addressing such issues as sexual behavior and men's ethics in today's society. *The Highest Education* supports all six CrossSeekers Covenant principles and focuses on the need for accountability as a key for young men to grow into Christian leaders of tomorrow. Each session provides testimonies of godly men found in Scripture, coupled with modern men found on today's college campuses.
♦ 6 sessions ♦ Leader's guide included ♦ $6.95
ISBN 0-6330-0457-X

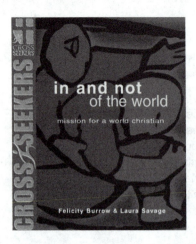

CrossSeekers: In And Not Of The World, Life Mission for a World Christian
by Felicity Burrow & Laura Savage
Service is a top priority in the hearts of many collegians today. This new study takes the desire for service and builds upon it by presenting the possibilities of Christian service and missions. It stresses the importance of mirroring the servant heart of Christ, and encourages such involvement as a transforming lifestyle during their college and young adult years.
• 6 sessions • Leader's helps included • $7.95
ISBN 0-7673-9088-1

CrossSeekers: Virtuous Reality, Becoming the Ideal Woman
by Vicki Courtney
Virtuous Reality challenges college women to become ideal women as defined by God's standards, rather than the world's standards. The primary Bible passage that forms the foundation of the book is Proverbs 31, which describes a virtuous woman with worth far above rubies. Sessions of the book attempt to dispel the world's definition of the ideal woman. They address key qualities of a virtuous woman and emphasize the importance of college women basing their worth solely on Christ. Sessions also challenge women to pursue wisdom, discern folly, develop a healthy perspective on dating, and discover their God-given purpose in life.
♦ 6 sessions ♦ Leader's guide included ♦ $6.95
ISBN 0-6330-0455-3

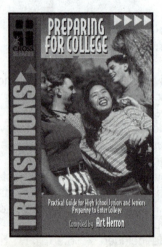

Transitions: Preparing for College
compiled by Art Herron
For high school juniors and seniors *and their parents*. Practical help for the transition from high school to college—the admissions process, financial aid, loans and scholarships, lifestyle changes, spiritual development, and more!
• 6 sessions • Leader's helps included • $7.95
ISBN 0-7673-9082-2

For more information, visit our Web site: www.crossseekers.org